Dream Castles

Dream Castles

by

MARY CABLE

"I am ruminating," said Mr. Pickwick, "on the strange mutability of human affairs."
"Ah! I see—in at the palace door one day, out at the window the next. Philosopher, sir?"
"An observer of human nature, sir," said Mr. Pickwick.

A Studio Book

THE VIKING PRESS

NEW YORK

To the memory of my mother,
Elizabeth Southwick Pratt

First published in 1966 by The Viking Press, Inc.
625 Madison Avenue, New York, N.Y. 10022

Published simultaneously in Canada by
The Macmillan Company of Canada Limited

Library of Congress catalog card number: 66-25277
Printed in U.S.A.

The text of this book first appeared,
in somewhat different form, in *Horizon*.

Contents

Ludwig's Dream Castles
Linderhof, Neuschwanstein, Herrenchiemsee

"THEY CALLED HIM THE CRAZY KING! WELL, I WILL TELL YOU something," the guide on the tourist bus confided into a loudspeaker. "The Crazy King was not crazy at all!"

We were parked alongside a souvenir-and-postcard stall in the grounds of Schloss Linderhof, the sumptuous hunting lodge built some eighty-five years ago in the Bavarian Alps by Ludwig II. Warm May weather had brought out sightseers, including a good many Bavarians in their native dress, and the atmosphere was festive, almost carnival. Souvenirs and postcards were selling briskly, and, at the outdoor restaurant nearby, so were beer and wurst.

The guide was a glum and discouraged-looking man, but now that he began to speak of Ludwig, a note of enthusiasm came into his voice. "He was against war, he was against Prussia, and he loved art—so they said he was crazy! He was also very religious—so religious that he could not marry anyone because he was secretly in love with his cousin, the Empress Elizabeth of Austria." Here the guide paused and, with something like royal disdain, looked at the apathetic tourist-faces before him. "Now we get out of the bus and we go through the castle. He hated crowds, the great king. He was a real Bavarian, he liked to go away to the mountains. In Munich they said he was so extravagant he must be crazy—but today the State of Bavaria can afford to keep up its other old castles because of the admission fees at Linderhof, Neuschwanstein, and Herrenchiemsee. So who's crazy? Don't touch anything and don't walk on the parquet."

The Bavarians, who love fairy tales, cherish this one—a potpourri of truth, fantasy, and speculation about King Ludwig. Although the real Ludwig, a stout, unhappy man, died at the age of forty in 1886, shortly after being taken in hand by psychiatrists, a fairy-tale Ludwig still survives: a tall, blue-eyed youth with dark

Ludwig II and his fiancée in 1867.

7

wavy hair, who did exactly what he pleased—which was to build castles. The three strange, resplendent castles he built, each grandly and remotely placed and glittering with riches, are so impractical as to be of use only to a fugitive from reality. Ludwig never intended them to be used in the ordinary sense: he had no queen and no children, never held any state dinners, balls, or receptions, and, since he never invited anyone to spend the night, needed but one bedroom to a castle (two in Herrenchiemsee, the extra one being intended for the mystical convenience of the long-dead Louis XIV of France). Today, all the royal apartments look nearly as pristine as they must have looked in the 1880s. There are no scratches, no worn carpets, no fragile springs. The rich colors of the draperies—violet, crimson, emerald, sky or lapis blue—have scarcely faded. Here and there the fabric is disintegrating, but only from time and the weight of gold embroidery, not from the touch of human fingers. These are enchanted castles, not meant for flesh and blood.

Ludwig does not seem to have had any creative talents himself, and he never sought any training in architecture or design. But he was adept at writing "approved" or "not approved" on the sketches of the many architects and designers who worked for him, and he supervised his castle-building down to the last doorknob, so that the over-all result reflects Ludwig and no one else. Everywhere are enigmatic clues to his personality: What sort of man, one wonders, would feel that he needed a throne of cast-zinc peacock feathers? Or a couch with mirrors at head and foot, so that he could see himself ad infinitum? Or a golden rococo sleigh drawn by four plumed horses in which to ride by moonlight all alone? A study of Ludwig's life explains some of this; the rest swirls away in a pretty mist of legend and fairy tale—and, perhaps, in the smoke of burned papers and letters. Why has Ludwig become a hero? We can only guess. Perhaps his countrymen, drilled from childhood in strict discipline and obedience, nourish a secret longing to jump over the moon and are delighted by a king who tried to do so.

Ludwig Friedrich Wilhelm Wittelsbach was born at Nymphenburg Palace, outside Munich, on August 25, 1845. His grandfather, first Ludwig in the line of Wittelsbach rulers of Bavaria, was then King: pleasure-loving, cultivated, willful, and not of great use to his country except as an importer of opera, art, and elegant manners, and as an embellisher of the city of Munich. The baby's father, Crown Prince Maximilian, was a more typical Bavarian: bourgeois in his tastes, conservative, and given to romanticism and flowery sentiment, provided these did not conflict too outrageously with common sense. Maximilian's consort was Marie of Prussia, a woman of not many brains but with normal control of those she had. Years later, it was said in Bavaria that the taint of insanity that afflicted both Ludwig and his younger brother Otto, who was hopelessly insane from boyhood, came from the Prussians, but the fact was that several Wittelsbachs had been locked away and that Ludwig I himself was a man of such ungoverned passions as to border on the pathological.

When Ludwig I was sixty-two years old, soon after the birth of his grandson, his eye lighted up at the sight of Lola Montez, the redoubtable Spanish dancer from Limerick, Ireland, and she became his acknowledged mistress. Emulating the Bourbon kings of France, whom he dearly loved to emulate, the aging King not only showered his mistress with jewels, money, and titles, but allowed her to hire and fire ministers of state. Unfortunately for Ludwig, the year 1848 was at hand, a bad one for kings, and this final nonsense was too much for the Bavarians. Ludwig's cabinet—called, by an indignant populace shouting in the streets, the *Lolaministerium*—resigned, and the King abdicated. Maximilian thereupon succeeded to the throne, and the infant Ludwig became Crown Prince.

The boy grew up in an environment that was strict, loveless, rigidly formal, and, at the same time, pervaded with rampant romanticism. King Max and Queen Marie bought Hohenschwangau, an old ruined castle in the Bavarian Alps, and set about restoring it to what they perhaps imagined was its original state. Because the medieval lords of Schwangau had had a swan on their escutcheon, Maximilian, carried away by the newly awakened Pan-Germanic enthusiasm for Middle High German lore, decided to link the castle with Lohengrin and ordered enormous murals for the royal apartments showing scenes from the Lohengrin legend. The furniture of the castle was Gothic, most of it pale ash. In his bedroom the King had murals of the love affair of Tasso's Rinaldo and Armida, and the ceiling was covered with stars and orange trees. As for the Queen, she fancied dreamy Oriental landscapes and Turkish knickknacks. Lohengrin's swan was embroidered on the draperies and chair seats, carved on the woodwork, engraved on the silver serving dishes, painted on the ceilings; and, of course, there were whole flotillas of swans adrift on the beautiful lake, the Schwansee, far below the castle windows. (One day, years later, Ludwig II was to push the swan motif even further by dressing a young man in Lohengrin armor and setting him forth on the lake in a swan boat.) The royal family was much attached to Hohenschwangau and spent several months of each year there.

From the age of eight, Ludwig had lessons all day long; for some reason, it had been decided that he would learn in five years what Bavarian school children learned in eight, and as he grew older he often studied from half past five in the morning until eight in the evening. The lesson he seems to have learned best was that, next to his father, he was the most important personage around. His governess one day was dismayed to find that he had stolen a small gaudy purse from a shop near the royal residence at Hohenschwangau. "But why have I done wrong?" he asked. "Why should it be a sin? One day I shall be king of this country, and all that belongs to my subjects belongs to me."

King Max died in 1864, and Ludwig, not yet nineteen years old, succeeded him. The young King was six-foot-three and strikingly handsome. The Bavarians, catching one of their first good views of him as he walked through the streets of Munich behind his father's coffin, were delighted with him. They clamored to see him more often, and the more they clamored, the more elusive he became. He feared crowds, disdained persons of common birth, and was happiest when by himself or watching a play or an opera (before long he began to combine these pleasures by having theatrical performances put on for him alone). He had seen *Lohengrin* for the first time when he was fifteen and apparently had jumped to the conclusion that a man who could bring heroes to life must necessarily be a hero, too, for one of his first acts as King was to seek out Richard Wagner—who was hard to find because he was hiding from creditors—and send for him, pay his debts, and provide him with a house in Munich, a castle on Lake Starnberg, and a comfortable income.

Ludwig himself does not seem to have been musical: after five years of piano lessons, his tutor had said there was no point in going on, because his Royal Highness the Crown Prince has "neither talent for music nor does he like it. . . ." It was not for music that he idolized Wagner but for the Wagnerian themes, and if the composer had set other stories to music, he would probably never have met the King of Bavaria. Ludwig's mind was drenched in fantasy, and his human relationships were significant to him only insofar as they helped make fantasy seem real. His obsession was to shut out the world of nineteenth-century Germany, where monarchs were bothered by niggling financial ministers, where a Prussian bully, Count Bismarck, was destroying Bavarian sovereignty, and where (even worse) no one talked in poetry, and rooms were stuffed with Biedermeier furniture. To Ludwig, a royal Miniver Cheevy, almost any other century looked better.

At first, he was graciously willing to take his people along with him on his magic carpet: one of his first big projects was a rococo opera house, to be built especially for the première of the complete *Ring des Nibelungen* cycle, and to stand in Munich on the bank of the Isar with a grand boulevard and bridge leading to it. But he soon began bitterly to realize that his governess had been right—it was not true that "whatever belongs to my subjects belongs to me." His finance minister denied him the money, and the architect who made the sketches was obliged to sue before he was paid for them. Munich, a city of 150,000, already had a large opera house and did not want a new one, especially one for Wagnerian operas. Richard Wagner was the most unpopular man in town. Except for Ludwig, royalists hated Wagner because he had been associated with the revolutionary movements of 1848 and was even rumored to have fought at the barricades in Dresden; socialists hated him because he was sheltered under the wing of a would-be absolute ruler; the ordinary citizenry cared nothing for politics, but was scandalized by Wagner's affair with Cosima von Bülow. Wagner was then fifty-one years old, and his amatory record included an abandoned wife and any number of mistresses, of whom Frau von Bülow was the latest. But the unworldly young King refused to listen to the clamorous gossip and stood by his hero. In fact, he wrote an open letter to the lady's husband, the noted conductor Hans von Bülow, which said, in part: "As I have been in a position to obtain the most intimate knowledge of the character of your honorable wife, it only remains for me to discover the inexplicable reasons for these criminal insults." But people began to call Wagner "Lolus," and the prime minister threatened to resign if Wagner did not leave Munich. Ludwig, the absolute monarch born too late, meekly sent Wagner to live in Switzerland.

Not long after, Ludwig learned beyond a shadow of a doubt that Wagner was indeed the lover of Cosima and the father of the third child in the Von Bülow family. Surprisingly, this did not destroy Ludwig's devotion to Wagner, but possibly it impelled him to seek out a relationship with a woman himself. Some months later, he became engaged to his first cousin once removed, Sophie, a pretty, docile Wittelsbach princess. (Gossip, however, insisted that he was in love with her elder sister, Elizabeth, Empress of Austria.) Ludwig called Sophie "Elsa," himself "Heinrich." "My dear Elsa!" he wrote to her, "The God of my life, as you know, is Richard Wagner" . . . "My beloved Elsa! . . . How happy I am to have seen Him again and talked to Him after nine long months" . . . "W. comes to me today at 1 o'clock and we shall have a couple of beautiful hours of cosy talk together; think of Us!" One wonders what Sophie thought of such love letters.

A wedding coach was ordered, painted with scenes of the life of Louis XIV plus a scene of a theater during a performance of a Wagner opera; Sophie was measured for a crown; an elaborate apartment, connected by secret staircase with Ludwig's, was prepared for her in the Munich *Residenz*. And during the blessedly long time that these things took, Ludwig went off incognito to Paris in the company of his chief groom. Twice the wedding date

The Grotto, with its fake rocks and stalactites. The backdrop of the Venusberg turns up again in Ludwig's study at Schloss Neuschwanstein.

The twelve-room Schloss Linderhof, whose chief
architect and decorator was a stage designer.

was postponed; the bride's father was forced to make indignant inquiries; and at last Ludwig wrote Sophie as honest a letter as was possible for him: "Now I have had time to test myself, and think the whole matter over, and I see that my true and faithful brotherly love is now, and always will be, deeply rooted in my soul; but I also see that there is not the love which is necessary for a matrimonial union." In his diary Ludwig noted: "Sophie written off. The gloomy picture fades. . . . Now I live again after this torturing nightmare."

Having closed the doors to a normal life, he was free to hurry down the secret passageways of his own fantastic world. Forthwith he plunged himself into the real passion of his life—building and decorating. His trip to France, where he had seen the Paris Exposition of 1867 as well as Versailles and other royal palaces, seems to have set his imagination flying off in all directions, and the architects' offices of Munich began to burn lights late into the night. Plans were drawn up for a facsimile of Versailles, for a medieval fortress with a Singers' Hall in it like the one in *Tannhäuser*, and for a Moorish-Byzantine palace. The royal apartments in the Munich *Residenz* were enlarged and decorated lavishly in a late-late-rococo style, and an enormous winter garden under a vaulted glass roof was added to the top floor of the *Residenz*, with palm trees, fountains, a pond and a running stream, a blue silk tent, a bamboo hut, a stalactite grotto, and an Oriental kiosk. There were stuffed swans and real peacocks, and a small barque for rowing about; and in the background, a painting of the Himalayas. A sturdy soprano who had come to the palace ostensibly to discuss a forthcoming opera, but who had hopes of bringing the aloof young man around to more personal subjects, once climbed aboard the barque, upset it, and screamed for help; Ludwig, instead of wading in and seizing her in his arms, rang for footmen and bade his damp visitor good night.

Schloss Linderhof, begun in 1869, started out to be a little country château like Marly, near Versailles, but when it was completed ten years later, it was pure Ludwigian. The chief of the architects and decorators was Christian Jank, a Munich stage designer, and certainly Linderhof looks more like a stage set than a place to live. It has only twelve rooms, excepting servants' quarters, and the outstanding impression they all convey is *horror vacui*. The modern eye rebels at the sight of so much clutter. But Ludwig, however much he deplored the taste of his time, was inevitably influenced by it; and if one looks at photographs of Ludwig's contemporaries —Queen Victoria in a sitting room at Sandringham that looks like the Old Curiosity Shop, or Kaiser Wilhelm competing for the photographer's attention with a welter of elk heads, ancestral portraits, Biedermeier sofas, Gothic armchairs, lace curtains, Oriental rugs, antlers, Meissen vases, and potted palms—one finds Ludwig's apartments restful. Everything, down to the last toothbrush holder, was designed for the exact place where it still stands. Each room is so like the next that one comes away with a blurred impression of dazzle and splendor, in which only a few bits stand out clearly—the life-sized porcelain peacock, the upright Aeolian piano strewn with gold rococo squiggles, or the canopy above the King's worktable, lined with ermine from the coronation robe of Ludwig's cousin Otto of Greece (this is the sole example anywhere in Ludwig's décor of thrift, or making-do, and one wonders if he minded the second hand ermine). Some of the paintings are on tapestry, to imitate Gobelin, and the subjects are mythological or allegorical— no German sagas here. Pastel portraits of Marie Antoinette, of Louis XIV, XV, and XVI, of Madame du Barry, Madame de Pompadour, and other French court figures bear identical bland, pudding-like expressions; it was the abstract idea of absolute monarchy that interested Ludwig, not nuances of personality.

By the time Linderhof was ready for Ludwig to live in, his manner of life was further than ever removed from reality. He arose at six or seven in the evening and had breakfast, dined at two hours past midnight, supped and retired at dawn. He liked to take his meals alone, but the table was usually set for three or four. Who were the unseen guests? Louis XIV was one, perhaps; a servant once came upon Ludwig saluting and talking to a statue of Louis XIV that stands in the main hallway of Linderhof. (Ludwig believed himself a spiritual heir of the Bourbons because his grandfather, Ludwig I, had been a godson of Louis XVI. He sometimes called Linderhof "Meicost Ettal," an anagram of *l'etat c'est moi.*) Often the ghostly dinner would take place at Ludwig's *Tischlein-deck-dich,* a table copied from one at Versailles that could pop into view, fully spread, by means of machinery that boosted it through the floor. The kitchen had always to be ready for sudden changes in the royal appetite. Ludwig liked kingly-looking food—peacock, for instance, stuffed with forcemeat and truffles and served up with its head and tail feathers. He expected dishes like this to be forthcoming when he wanted them and thought nothing of advancing or retarding dinner without consideration of the cooks' nerves. Sometimes he would suddenly decide to dine on a perch amid the branches of a large lime tree in the garden; or in a mountain hut; or at the Schachen, a hunting lodge designed in a curious blend of Swiss chalet and Turkish kiosk; or in one of several outbuildings that he constructed on the Linderhof grounds—the Moorish kiosk, Hunding's Hut, or the Grotto.

Hunding's Hut (destroyed in 1945) was a replica in-the-round of a stage set for the first act of *Die Walküre*. In the middle was a living ash tree, pierced by a replica of Siegfried's sword. For the rest, there were many antlers and bearskins, and when the King was in a jovial frame of mind, he and a few favored courtiers would lie about dressed as early Teutons and drink mead out of horns. Game was their principal food; silver jugs in the shape of deer held cream for the coffee—which would doubtless have surprised Siegfried—and the salt and pepper shakers were shaped like little owls.

When the Teutonic mood was not upon him, Ludwig had a penchant for the Oriental. In 1867, at the Paris Exposition, he had bought a Moorish kiosk, the property of a bankrupt millionaire from Bohemia, and this was eventually set up at Linderhof. The kiosk was not particularly Moorish, having been conceived and built in Berlin of pressed zinc plaques. But Ludwig was enchanted with it and installed a throne in the shape of a huge zinc peacock, its tail feathers enameled and set with glittering Bohemian glass. Next to swans, peacocks were the favorite bird of the King, and he cherished a desire to be drawn about by peacocks harnessed to a small gilded car, as he had heard was done in ancient Persia; he even wrote to the incumbent Shah of Persia, asking for a shipment of sturdy peacocks along with training instructions. No peacocks arrived, but he enjoyed lolling on his peacock throne and drinking a *bowle* made by soaking violet roots in champagne, accompanied by *petits fours* and candied violets.

But of all the phantasmagoria at Linderhof, the Grotto is the strangest. The inspiration for the Grotto came partly from the Blue Grotto in Capri, partly from the Venus Grotto, where Tannhauser drank the cup of oblivion, and partly from Ludwig's father's bathroom at Hohenschwangau. The latter had been hollowed out of the rock on which the castle stands; it was lit by a red light in the ceiling and was entered by pressing a secret spring in a slab of papier-mâché rock. Ludwig's artificial grotto at Linderhof opens in the same manner, but outdoes the paternal bathroom in almost every other way. It is several hundred feet long, fifty feet high, and is not made of rock at all, but of brick and iron clothed in canvas and cement to make them look like rocks and stalagmites. It also contains a lake, which the King sometimes swam in and sometimes rowed about on, in a gilded, shell-shaped boat. A waterfall gurgles noisily down from the bogus rocks, and in Ludwig's day artificial waves could be whipped up on the lake's surface by means of a small machine. Dim, varicolored lights and a luminous rainbow were provided by the first electricity plant in Bavaria, erected on an adjacent slope, and twenty-five dynamos (then very recently invented). Back of the lake, a huge painting depicts Act I of *Tannhäuser* and swarms of cherubs and fairies. The whole place must have seemed very recherché to the King, but to a modern eye it is unfortunately reminiscent of a Coney Island fun house.

But if the Grotto is ridiculous, Ludwig was occasionally capable of the sublime. And if he ever achieved a triumph of creative imagination, it was in choosing the site for the castle of Neuschwanstein. It stands among monumental gray crags, with snowy Alps above, a green plain below, and the lovely little jade-green lakes of Schwansee and Alpsee not far away. One wonders if, in building it, Ludwig did not set out to outdo his father, for the windows of this castle look down on Hohenschwangau, which in comparison is only the restored fortress of a petty lord. The architects of Neuschwanstein worked from sketches made by the same scene designer who worked on Linderhof, and probably no professional architect would have arrived at such a never-never look for solid stone and brickwork. During the construction, Ludwig was often on hand to supervise the workmen personally; but the royal apartments took so long to build and decorate that he was able to occupy them only for less than half a year.

Unhappily, the castle interior is less felicitous than its exterior. Romanesque, Early Gothic, Tudor, Moorish, and Byzantine architecture and decorations are chucked together with a heavy hand, and everywhere are those outsized insipid paintings that could only be nineteenth century. Tristan and Isolde, Lohengrin and Elsa, Walther and Eva, and other heroes and heroines of Middle High German poetry command the walls, looking noble, vacuous, and stiff as pokers. Never was so much love celebrated with so little reference to sex. In a painting showing Tannhäuser on the Venusberg, which dominates the King's study, Venus is as naked as, but no more sensual than, a billiard ball, while Tannhäuser, fully clothed, sits at her feet and looks as if he might be thinking out a chess problem. Then there are the usual Ludwigian touches: a bathroom full of artificial stalactites (what was this family passion for bathing in a cave?), a porcelain vase in the shape of a full-sized swan, and a carved oak bed-canopy in late Gothic style that is a perfect forest of turrets, ogives, and pinnacles. Ludwig always gave most attention to the royal bedroom, which he regarded as a symbol of monarchy. Louis XIV had received courtiers, ministers, and sundry callers in bed, and Ludwig may have intended to copy him, but as he grew older he rarely received anyone. The last room added to Neuschwanstein was a throne room, which, like so much else in Ludwig's castles, was of no use at all. The theme is Byzantine, for, more and more, Ludwig was drawn to the Byzantine concept

Culver Pictures, Inc.

ABOVE: One of the painted walls in the king's study, Schloss Neuschwanstein, depicting Tannhäuser on the Venusberg.

of royalty as near-deity. The throne itself, which was to be of ivory and pure gold, never materialized; above the empty space reserved for it are murals—painted to resemble mosaic—depicting six canonized kings of Christendom and, above them, the risen Christ with Saint John and the Virgin, so that the room seems something like a church. This is the most theatrical-looking of all Ludwig's rooms, perhaps because the paintings are faked mosaics and the pillars, supposed to look like porphyry and lapis lazuli, are too red and too blue and are obviously only plaster. By the time Ludwig planned the throne room, his sight was weakening, and, being a very vain man, he would not wear glasses; also, because of his peculiar schedule, he rarely saw anything by light brighter than candle or moon. At any rate, he must by this time have felt something like an actor who, by walking onto a stage, seems to turn it into a real world, while the commonplace life of the pit and the stalls fades into darkness and hush.

*   *   *

Ludwig's third *Schloss,* Herrenchiemsee, inspired by and partly copied from Versailles, stands on a small island in the Chiemsee, one of the largest of the Bavarian Alpine lakes. The cornerstone was laid in 1878 and building continued, to the tune of twenty million marks, until 1885, when the state treasury put a stop to it, leaving some twenty rooms finished and sumptuously decorated and the rest of the palace no more than bare bricks and plaster. These royal rooms, lighted by thousands of white candles in more than a hundred crystal, ivory, or porcelain chandeliers, are an extraordinary sight, a sight that Ludwig is said to have seen only once, when he walked from room to room all alone. By day, when Ludwig never saw the palace, it looks gaudy and overdone and reminds one all too plainly how difficult it is for a man to escape his century. The great entrance hall is meticulously copied after the Ambassadors' Staircase at Versailles; yet the unsubtle colors of the ubiquitous heroic paintings, the staring-white stucco, and the disastrous idea of adding a glass roof (suggesting Waterloo Station), mark it inexorably as a work of the late nineteenth century. Dissatisfied with the empty appearance of Louis XIV's Hall of Mirrors, Ludwig supplied his version with 47 banquettes, 12 tabourets, 52 candelabras, 8 orange trees in specially designed tubs, 4 vases, 16 busts of classical emperors, and 33 chandeliers. The painted figures that swarm across the ceiling have been provided here and there with stucco legs and arms, which make them look as if they were wildly trying to struggle free of the ceiling. This whimsy of Bavarian eighteenth-century rococo would have dismayed a seventeenth-century Frenchman and imparts a slightly berserk appearance to this Hall of Mirrors.

Ludwig slept in his costly palace exactly nine nights, from September 7 to 16, 1885. He himself said that he had intended it less as a dwelling than a temple, a shrine dedicated to the Sun King, Louis XIV, and to the idea of Absolutism. The most important and most expensive room in the palace is the bedroom for the symbolic use of Louis XIV, modeled after the royal bedroom at Versailles but larger and far more elaborate. Ludwig supplied the ghost of his idol with a golden railing to separate the bed from the rest of the room—an old Bavarian idea, not French at all. He also gave Louis a gilt bowl and pitcher big enough for a giant, hangings of dark-red velvet that took twenty women seven years to encrust with gold embroidery, a parquet floor intricately inlaid with rose-wood, and a tapestry-painting showing Louis XIV with his ancestor Saint Louis and—unobtrusively standing in the background—his spiritual descendant, Ludwig.

Ludwig's own bedroom is comparatively modest. The draperies are blue, the color Ludwig preferred in all his bedrooms, and there is a giant blue globe at the foot of the bed to serve as a night light. Here, as in every bedroom he planned for himself, is a curious juxtaposition of religious and amorous symbols. At the head of the bed is an embroidery depicting Louis XIV triumphing over Vice, while at the foot is a carved relief of Venus set between fully modeled figures of Cupid and Psyche.

Although Herrenchiemsee was not nearly finished, Ludwig set about planning more castles. There was to be a Byzantine palace, a robber-baron eyrie on a higher and less accessible crag than Neuschwanstein, and a walled Chinese palace where the court was to adopt the dress and ceremonial of mandarins. There was one rather large stumbling block: money. The King's credit was no longer good anywhere, and he owed ten million marks. When a moneylender came forward with the offer of a four-hundred-thousand-mark loan in return for a title, Ludwig, though he eventually gave in, at first refused indignantly: Did they suppose the King had no honor? His advisers pleaded with him. Where else, they asked, could the money be found? "Steal it!" cried Ludwig.

* * *

Early in the morning of Thursday, June 10, 1886, a delegation of ministers of state, accompanied by a noted psychiatrist, Dr. Bernhard von Gudden, and several skilled male nurses, arrived at the gatehouse of Neuschwanstein. They brought with them a parliamentary order to place the King under medical care. There was a clause in the Bavarian constitution stating that a king incapable of carrying out his proper duties could be relieved of them and replaced by a regency; that Ludwig was incapable seemed so apparent that four psychiatrists, none of whom had ever seen the

Edwin N. Beery, M.D.

ABOVE: Schloss Herrenchiemsee, on a small island in one of the largest lakes in the Bavarian Alps. RIGHT: The Hall of Mirrors at Herrenchiemsee; though an imitation of the Hall of Mirrors at Versailles, it tries to outdo Louis XIV with its 52 candelabras, 33 chandeliers, and other embellishments.

King, had signed a report declaring him insane. In addition to his unreasoning demands for money and his paralyzing effect on the orderly processes of government (when papers required the royal signature, ministers often had to meet the King in some remote mountain rendezvous where, in the middle of the night, Ludwig would arrive by coach-and-four, hurriedly sign the papers with his now illegible "Ludwig" and whirl away again), there was a stack of evidence obtained from his servants: that they must approach the King on their bellies, that he had them physically chastised and bound, that he talked to trees and embraced a certain pillar at Linderhof each time he passed it, and that he complained of terrible pressure in his head, sometimes so severe that he had to come to meals wearing an ice pack.

22

The members of the commission from Munich had not brought military support with them, and, to their annoyance, they found that the King's loyal guard would not let them into Neuschwanstein. There was nothing for them to do but withdraw to the nearest village and wonder what to do next. They had not long to wonder: within the hour a company of gendarmes arrived from the King with orders to arrest them. In vain they showed the captain of gendarmes a paper stating that Prince Luitpold, the King's uncle, was already Regent; finally they consented to the indignity of being locked up in the Neuschwanstein gatehouse. The King now issued a series of five orders that at last shook the faith of his supporters. The orders were (1) skin the members of the commission alive, (2) scalp them, cut off their tongues and hands, and flog them to death, (3) blind them, (4) place them in heavy chains, and (5) fling them into a deep dungeon to starve to death. Afterwards the captain of gendarmes admitted that if the royal order had simply directed him to shoot all members of the commission, he would unhesitatingly have carried it out. As it was, he and his assistants debated for several hours before deciding to try to get instructions from the government in Munich.

Before all the red tape had been cut and Dr. Gudden was finally free to try to take charge of his patient, two more days had passed, and Ludwig was drinking heavily, threatening suicide, and calling for the keys to the highest tower of Neuschwanstein. Dr. Gudden stationed male nurses on the tower stairway and then had the keys sent to Ludwig. Ludwig immediately made for the tower, was taken, and then driven in a locked carriage to the small *Schloss* of Berg, on Lake Starnberg—an eight-hour drive from Neuschwanstein—which was to be made over into a one-patient mental hospital.

The last of Ludwig's pathetic story will never be known for certain. The day after the arrival at Berg, Ludwig, who was behaving in a fairly quiet and docile manner, consented to go for an evening walk along the lakeside with Dr. Gudden. Neither was ever seen alive again. Through a misunderstanding, no attendant followed the two: the doctor had probably expected to be followed at a discreet distance, while the attendant had understood that he was not to come at all. The body of Dr. Gudden was found in shallow water; he had drowned, and there were bruises and marks of strangulation on his neck. The body of the King was found farther out in the lake, in water less than four feet deep. He had been an excellent swimmer, so whether he had drowned himself or had suffered a heart attack and collapsed in the water will always be a mystery. A wooden cross, often garlanded with fresh flowers, marks the place where he died.

A Habitable Monument

Blenheim Palace

EVERY NATION HAS ITS MEMORIALS TO NATIONAL HEROES:
tombs, arches, statues, squares, bridges, and *in memoriam* public
works of every kind punctuate history, from the Pyramids to the
Pulaski Skyway. But rare—possibly unique—is the notion of a
monument in which the hero's descendants are invited to live, eat,
have babies, pay taxes, and make repairs until the end of time.
Such a monument is Blenheim Palace, which Queen Anne, in 1705,
ordered to be erected as "a proper means for perpetuating the
memory of the great services performed by the Duke of Marlborough."

Some two hundred and fifty years have passed and Blenheim
is still standing, a majestic exercise in English baroque that con-
trasts somewhat startlingly with the simple green countryside all
around it; it could be a bank or a public library, inexplicably
dropped there among the peaceable meadows. Certainly it does not
look a comfortable place to live in; but, notwithstanding, it still
serves its intended dual purpose. While respectful tourists mill
through some of the 187 rooms, amid battle flags, tapestries, paintings, and statues, all testifying to the glory of the First Duke, the
Tenth Duke and his family carry on as best they can in one wing,
their presence discreetly suggested by a television aerial that peeps up
among Grinling Gibbons' carving on the roof top.

The palace, standing in the middle of extensive formal gardens, covers seven acres. Horace Walpole called it "a quarry of
stone," and for Voltaire it was "*une grosse masse de pierre, sans
agrément et sans gout.*" On the other hand, Sir Joshua Reynolds
admired the way the architect, Sir John Vanbrugh, had, like a
painter, "marshalled his masses and proportioned his light and
shade." Daniel Defoe, who visited Blenheim in 1742, wrote, "It
requires the Royalty of a Sovereign Prince to support an Equipage

suitable to the Greatness of this Palace." And King George III,
who stopped there as the guest of the Fourth Duke, remarked
crossly, "We have nothing to equal this."

But beauty and grandeur are not the most striking qualities
of this palace: its seven-foot-thick walls (weathered now to a
rather ugly, yellowish dark-gray), its massive columns, its gigantic
windows, its disdain for any kind of moderation, bespeak
nothing so much as power, pride, and ambition. It is as if Blenheim's three creators, the Duke and Duchess of Marlborough and
Sir John Vanbrugh, had managed to build their own personalities
into it. Sir John wanted it to be the crown of his career; the
Duchess, though she said she hated Blenheim, for love of her hus-

RIGHT: Anne, Queen of Great Britain and Ireland. CENTER: John Churchill, first Duke of Marlborough, K.G. FAR RIGHT: Sarah Churchill, Duchess of Marlborough, from the original of Sir Peter Lely in the collection of the Duke of Marlborough.

Brown Brothers

band and her husband's glory "worked like a pack horse" (her
words) to see it finished; and Marlborough himself saw in it a
mystical means of transmuting his glory into permanent form. Sir
Winston Churchill, in *Marlborough, His Life and Times,* has
tried to explain his ancestor's point of view: "Marlborough had set
his heart upon this mighty house in a strange manner . . . It was as
a monument, not as a dwelling, that he so earnestly desired it. Hence
the enormous thickness of the walls and masses of masonry in
Vanbrugh's plan had appealed to him, and had probably been suggested by him. As the Pharoahs built their Pyramids, so he sought
a physical monument which would certainly stand, if only as a
ruin, for thousands of years. About his achievements he preserved
a complete silence, offering neither explanations nor excuses for any
of his deeds. His answer was to be this great house." Another
descendant, the Ninth Duke of Marlborough, put it this way: "It

seemed to him [Marlborough] a special mercy of Providence that his talents should be placed at the disposal of England and not of any other country. . . . That such a boon should pass without formal thanks offended his sense of piety. Therefore he set himself to see that his exploits were worthily commemorated, and took it as a matter of course that no memorial could be too magnificent."

At the time of his greatest achievement, the victory at the Bavarian village of Blindheim ("Blenheim") in 1704, John Churchill, Duke of Marlborough, was fifty-four years old and had been a successful military man and courtier since the days of Charles II. He and his Duchess, Sarah, both the children of obscure gentlemen, had married at Charles's intrigueful court, bringing each

Brown Brothers

Bettmann Archive. Inc.

other no money but a wealth of wit, brains, charm, good looks, ability, and shrewd judgment, all dedicated to getting ahead. They also seemed to have an enviable knack for staying on the winning side. Young Churchill's first military successes were in the service of his future enemy, Louis XIV; he became a general and a baron under James II—the Earl of Marlborough under James's deposers, William and Mary. Sarah, since childhood, had been the favorite friend of James's daughter, Princess Anne, and when several unexpected turns of fate brought that mousy princess to the throne, Sarah and her husband became the most powerful persons in the realm.

In the same month that Anne was crowned—April 1702—England, allied with Austria, the Netherlands, and several German principalities, went to war against France and Spain, and at the head of the English troops rode Marlborough. By the following winter, the allies had won several important victories. The

Queen made Marlborough a duke. Revenues followed, but after the most glorious victory of Blenheim, Anne was momentarily at a loss to know what more to bestow. Would the Duke like a square in London named for him, with a statue in the middle and a great town house to overlook it? No, was Sarah's opinion; he was a man of simple tastes and longed to settle in some peaceful, rustic corner. It was then that the Queen bethought herself of the royal estate of Woodstock, near Oxford. There was a five-hundred-year-old manor there, known to history because it had been inhabited in the twelfth century by Fair Rosamund, the mistress of Henry II, and in the sixteenth by Elizabeth I, who had been imprisoned there as a young princess by her sister Mary. The manor had been partly ruined during the Cromwellian wars; ruins not yet being in fashion. Queen Anne proposed to tear them down, build a palace for the nation's greatest hero, and rearrange the landscape.

On March 14, 1705, the Queen sanctioned a bill that had passed both Houses granting the manor and land at Woodstock to Marlborough. All he and his descendants were to do in return was to send a French standard to the reigning sovereign on each anniversary of the Battle of Blenheim—a formality that is still carried out. No mention of money was made in the Parliamentary grant. The Queen sent it to the Board of Works with an order to erect at royal expense a splendid palace to be called the Castle of Blenheim. How much "royal expense" was not stated, but no one then imagined that the royal purse would ever snap shut where the Marlboroughs were concerned.

The Duke himself selected John Vanbrugh as the architect, passing over a more obvious choice, the aged Sir Christopher Wren. Vanbrugh, whom Marlborough had met at the Kit-Cat Club, was being talked of in fashionable London as the most inspired new architect on the scene. A baker's son from Chester, he had had a successful career as a playwright before turning his hand to architecture at the age of thirty-five. So far, he had completed only one building, a sumptuous opera house in Haymarket, which unfortunately, turned out to have wretched acoustics. He was working on a country seat for Lord Carlisle, to be known as Castle Howard, and Marlborough, much taken with the Castle Howard designs, asked Vanbrugh to submit proposals for Blenheim. This Vanbrugh speedily did, producing a model, "very large, exact, and intelligible," with which both Marlborough and the Queen were enchanted. The Queen asked Sir Christopher Wren to estimate the cost of such a building, and Sir Christopher's answer of "close to one hundred thousand pounds" did not dismay her.

Forthwith a thousand workmen were assembled at Woodstock, and just over three months from the date of Parliament's grant, a gigantic cornerstone, inscribed "In memory of the battle of Blenheim, June 18, 1705, Anna Regina," was ceremonially struck with a hammer by "seven gentlemen" and laid in the newly turned country earth. Music and morris dances followed the ceremony, with sack and claret for the gentry and plenty of cakes and ale for the common folk. Fortunately for the success of this party, no one had an inkling of the troubles that lay ahead.

In the summer of 1705, the palace site at Blenheim was as busy as an anthill. There was only one difficulty: nobody was getting paid. At first there were not many grumbles, as workmen and tradesmen in those days were accustomed to being kept waiting by their betters. But no one seemed to know for whose money they were waiting. Parliament had voted none; the Queen had said that the palace was to be a royal gift, but there was no sign of royal pounds and shillings; Vanbrugh, a few days before the cornerstone was laid, had taken the precaution of obtaining from the Treasurer, Lord Godolphin, a warrant that appointed him surveyor and contractor for the buildings at Woodstock "at the request and desire" and "on behalf" of the Duke of Marlborough, who "hath resolv'd to erect a large Fabrick, for a Mansion House." This document might be construed as making Marlborough responsible for the building of the Queen's present, and Vanbrugh locked it away against the off-chance that he should ever have to press for payment.

The bills at Blenheim piled up alarmingly. It was early discovered that the freestone quarried in Woodstock Park, which had been counted on for the walls of the palace, was neither of sufficient quantity nor of the best quality (frost caused it to "fly"), so that an unexpected amount of time, effort, and money had to be spent on dragging stone from quarries that were twenty to twenty-five miles away. The roads were bad or nonexistent, and the carters, who were also local farmers, had a way of disappearing when their farms needed attention.

Sir Christopher had not included in his estimate the price of the gardens or anything to be built therein, such as grottoes, bridges, walls, fountains, and sundials; yet it soon became apparent that both Vanbrugh and Marlborough were as much interested in the gardens as in the house. From the battlefields of Germany, His Grace wrote wistfully: "Pray press on my house and gardens . . . [it] would be a great pleasure to me at my return if I could see the walks in the park planted. . . . If possible I should wish that you might taste the fruit of every tree, so that what is not good might be changed." For Vanbrugh, the gardens were an integral part of the grand design and had to be laid out while the palace was going up. The rich earth dug spadeful by spadeful from the foundations was carefully assigned to various places in the garden. Henry Wise, the Queen's gardener, who was in charge of the operations, performed the then extraordinary feat of bringing full-grown trees to Woodstock Park in huge baskets and putting them into the ground, baskets and all. The formal gardens were to cover seventy-seven acres, and only the far corners of the two thousand acres of park were to be left wild.

Wise planned the position of each tree in the "woodwork" symmetrically, ruthlessly cutting down ancient oaks if they failed to fall in with his plan; the trees along the main approach to the palace he arranged to represent troop positions at Blenheim. The river Glyme, which meandered through the estate, he firmly channeled into a canal and studded with small, geometrically placed islands; part of it he dammed into a lake, from which spilled a short cascade. Over the Glyme, Vanbrugh threw an astonishing bridge, containing—for no known reason—thirty-three rooms and a catacomb of passages and dark stairways. Wise carried out his tremendous, ill-paid job splendidly. What he could not help was that formal parterres and neatly barbered woodlands were about to go out of style, and that following generations would destroy nearly all his painstaking work.

The gardening bills were enormous: "831 large flowering shrubs for the Woodwork Quarters at 6d. each"; "5,900 of Hornbeam, privatt, and Sweet Bryer for the Inner line of the woodwork at 1½ d."; "18,500 Dutch yellow crocus at 1s. 6d. a hundred"; "a thousand flowerpots, £6 17s. 7d."; "1,120 solid yards of Dung, £126." And the more the bills piled up, the more infrequently flowed the money. From time to time, Lord Godolphin, who was a great friend of the Marlboroughs and the father-in-law of one of their daughters, managed to channel some cash in the direction of Blenheim; but by 1707 the workmen were owed twenty thousand pounds, the palace was far from finished, and—what was really discouraging—Vanbrugh had taken to tearing down some of what was already built, as new inspirations came to him. He even decided, after two years of building, to change the architectural order from Doric to Corinthian, a fairly major alteration which meant much demolition and considerable increase in the building's height and ornamentation. The Duke began to fear that his age and infirmities would prevent him from ever enjoying his new home.

Between battles, he went shopping in The Hague for curtain materials: "There are seventeen pieces of the enclosed pattern, fourteen Dutch ells in each piece," he wrote. "Three or four of the pieces are damaged. However, they will not sell them unless they be all bought. They are contented to take £10 the Dutch ell, which

The main entrance of Blenheim, showing the colossal scale of Sir John Vanbrugh's work. The center block contains the private quarters; one wing houses the kitchens and store-

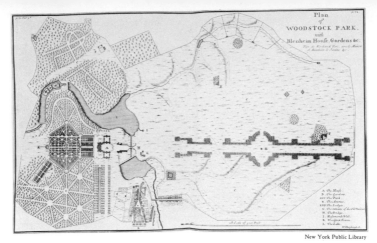

ABOVE: The original scheme of the gardens designed by Henry Wise.
The avenue of trees represents the disposition of troops at the Battle of
Blenheim. BELOW: Aerial view of Blenheim, "an Italian palace in an
English park," showing the water terraces and lake.

houses, and a second wing the stables. It may be a "habitable monument," but Vanbrugh was concerned more with the outward aspect than with the comfort of the inhabitants.

will make the whole come to one hundred and nineteen pounds. I desire you will let me know what use you can make of this velvet, and if you would have me buy it. I also send my coat-of-arms as they are to be on the hangings now making at Brussels, so that I desire you will send for Vanbrugh, and that he should take care that the crown and arms in the hangings already come over be exactly as this is."

Two more years went by and there was still no place at Blenheim for a duke to lay his head. There was a thirty-ton *busto* of Louis XIV, abstracted from the city gate of Tournai by Marlborough's troops and set up with infinite trouble above the south portico, where it still remains; there was a Bernini fountain, shipped to the Duke by the Spanish ambassador to Rome; there was a throng of fantastic carvings, some thirty feet high, by Grinling Gibbons; and the gardens were lavishly equipped with sundials. But when the Duchess paid "the great Digg" a visit, she had to climb into the main body of the palace by means of a ladder, as there were as yet no steps.

And if Marlborough's "greatest weakness" (as his wife said) was Blenheim, Vanbrugh's appears to have been the ruined manor of Woodstock, for instead of tearing it down, as he had more than once been told to do, he was living in it and spending time and money restoring it. By 1709 he had spent (that is, incurred debts for, since at Blenheim cash seldom changed hands) more than two thousand pounds on the manor. In valuing ruins, Vanbrugh was

LEFT: The Great Hall is adorned with battle flags taken at the Battle of Blenheim in Bavaria in 1704, when the English, under the Duke of Marlborough, with the Austrians, defeated the French and the Bavarians. OPPOSITE PAGE: The water terraces, on the west side, were laid out by the French landscape architect Duchêne, during the time of the ninth Duke (1871-1934).

The Times of London

ahead of his time, for a generation or two later any nobleman in England would have been glad of a well preserved and historic ruin on his property; but in 1709 a ruin was generally regarded as an eyesore, and the Marlboroughs and Lord Godolphin descended on Vanbrugh and ordered him to demolish the old manor at once. But Vanbrugh could not bring himself to obey. From 1709 until he resigned from the Blenheim job in 1716, he furtively restored wainscot ceilings and buttressed tumbling walls, and whenever the Duchess or her henchmen prowled near, he would hastily detail some workmen to make a show of pulling down one of Woodstock's outbuildings.

The Duke was nearly always in Flanders, and Sarah had to contend singlehanded with "Mr. Vanbrugh's madnesse" and with a Queen whose attitude toward both Marlboroughs had gradually turned from warm to chilly, and who therefore avoided discussion of their unpaid-for palace. Though the Duke won new victories in Europe (Ramillies, Oudenarde, Tournai, Malplaquet), the Queen blamed him for not managing to bring about peace. Her new favorite, Mrs. Masham, did not bully her as the Duchess of Marlborough was wont to do or outshine her in wit and intelligence.

In the spring of 1710, the Duchess had a stormy interview

with the Queen, after which she was never received again. Nevertheless, the advent of sunny summer weather saw work going forward with encouraging vigor at Blenheim: plasterers, joiners, and carpenters took over the interior shell of the house, the great arch of the bridge was keyed, and the gardens and the roof tops accumulated more of those impractical furbelows that drove the Duchess frantic—including (for the roof) four gilded copper balls, each twelve feet in diameter and weighing half a ton, and bringing with them a bill from a London coppersmith for £325 3s. 6d.

Then, suddenly, in August Queen Anne fired her Treasurer, Lord Godolphin; with him went the Blenheim workers' chief chance of reimbursement. Hopefully, they looked to the Marlboroughs; but in October 1710 Sarah gave orders to "put a stop at once to all sorts of work" until the Treasury should provide funds. Vanbrugh protested to the Duke, who was in Europe, and the Duke wrote his wife a chiding letter: "It no way becomes you or me to be giving orders for the Queen's money. . . . You know my opinion, that neither you, nor I, nor any of our friends ought to meddle in their accounts [the workmen's and tradesmen's] but to let it be taken by the Queen's officers as they always ought to be. . . . I think that those that take care of the building at Blenheim, when the winter season and the want of money makes the work to cease, should take care to cover the works, so as what is already done may receive no prejudice, and then it may remain as a *monument of ingratitude*, as Mr. Van. calls it in his letter."

The distress of the workmen was great; some of their families were actually starving, and others were being taken away to debtors' prison. A letter of the period says, "It will go hard with many in this town. . . . Their creditors begin to call on them and they can get no money at Blenheim." But the Duchess would not part with a penny of Marlborough money; and after some delay, the new Lord Treasurer, fearful of public opinion and of the possibility that the Duke would resign before the Queen was ready to dismiss him, asked Vanbrugh how much would be needed to "cover in" the unfinished work. Vanbrugh's answer was "at least eight thousand pounds"; the Treasury provided seven thousand.

In January 1711 the Queen relieved the Duchess of Marlborough of all her duties at court and in May requested that she move out of the apartments in St. James's Palace which had been hers for years. Sarah was subject to temper tantrums, and she had one now. Ordering the doorknobs and brass locks which she had herself installed in her rooms to be ripped out and packed with her effects, she left a shambles behind her. The Queen then declared that she would build no house for the Duke of Marlborough when the Duchess pulled hers to pieces. But in spite of every indication that

Blenheim was doomed to remain "a heap of stones," the Duke, during one of his brief winter visits to England, went down to Blenheim and studied the whole desolate scene with Vanbrugh. The dejected old Duke was loath to renounce his "greatest weakness," and as for Vanbrugh, one of his strongest qualities was optimism: "I was not one of those who drop their Spirits on every Rebuff; if I had, I had been under ground long ago." Together, they worked out an ambitious program for the coming season's work: the bridge was to be completed, the porticoes provided with steps, and the Hall, the Saloon, and all of the eastern portion of the building were to be finished inside.

The Lord Treasurer now asked Vanbrugh for an estimate of how much money was needed to finish Blenheim. Vanbrugh quoted £87,000, but added that he was omitting many items that he felt the Duke would pay for himself. That was in June; in August, £20,000 reached Blenheim, enough to pay the oldest debts and encourage the workmen to take up their picks and shovels. The Duchess came down from London occasionally and quarreled with Vanbrugh: one or the other of them was constantly ordering alterations in the private apartments. The plasterers finished the ceilings in the Duke's bedroom and dressing room, and then were instructed to pull them down; the stone chosen by Vanbrugh for the portico steps was found to be unsuitable, and the porticoes were left stepless for five more years.

Perhaps the chief cause of the muddle at Blenheim was that the Duke, the Duchess, and John Vanbrugh each had a different conception of what the palace should be. The Duke wanted a habitable monument; the Duchess, a comfortable country house; while Vanbrugh saw in his mind's eye a masterpiece of art, in which the bridge, the parterres, and the copper balls on the roof top were more important to the glorious whole than plaster in Her Grace's bedroom—so why should not plastering be left till last?

On the last day of December 1711 Queen Anne dismissed the Duke of Marlborough from all his duties. The news was a shock to Englishmen everywhere, but to none more so than to the workmen at Blenheim. Most of them left in despair; the few who stayed on, "trusting the building," made hay in the parterres and fished in the Glyme, while they quarreled, complained, and waited in vain for money. Vanbrugh was busy with more lucrative jobs; but whenever he could, he went to Blenheim, which he loved "with the Tendernesse of a sort of Childe of my owne," and could never forbear to make a few more improvements in the old ruined manor that he was supposed to be tearing down.

The Marlboroughs spent much of this time traveling abroad. Just as they were returning to England, on August 1, 1714, Queen

LEFT: The doorways in the Saloon are by Grinling Gibbons, the murals by Laguerre. RIGHT: On the wall of the Red Drawing Room hangs a portrait of the fourth Duke and his family, painted by Sir Joshua Reynolds in 1778.

Anne died. In September, George I arrived from Hanover to take over his new throne and received Marlborough with enthusiasm. "My Lord Duke," he said, "I hope your troubles are now all over." George arranged for one third of the Blenheim debts to be paid by the Treasury; and the Duke, on being informed by Vanbrugh that it would cost £54,000 more to finish the palace, decided to pay for it out of his own pocket.

In 1716 the battle that had been raging for years between the Duchess and Vanbrugh (now "Sir John" by grace of George I) came to its moment of decision. Sarah had always thought Vanbrugh too extravagant, resented the fact that he rarely did as she asked, and regarded as "madnesse" such whimseys as the thirty-three-room bridge and the putting up and tearing down of columns and ceilings as if they were no more than cardboard stage scenery. Now, paying a surprise visit to Woodstock Manor, she was appalled to discover what he had been up to there. He, for his part, was tired of what he called the Duchess's "Far-fetched, Labour'd Accusations, Mistaken Facts, Wrong Inferences, Groundless Jealousies, and strained Constructions." He resigned.

"I really believe," wrote Sarah, "that anybody that has sense . . . could make a better house without an architect than any has been built these many years." The Duke was ill and nearly helpless, having suffered two strokes; and Sarah, though she had never liked nor wanted Blenheim, now threw herself into the job of finishing it. First she sent for a plan of work-in-progress and re-

ceived one covered with discouraging notations: "nothing done," "no floors," "chimney pieces wanting," "no pavement," "the great stairs to make." And this, eleven years after that happy, morris-dancing day when the foundation stone was laid! Sarah wrote afterward that there was "no one room in the main body of the House in such a Condition as to put up a bed in it. . . . This thousands of people know that saw it in 1716, and Some of them said it was a Chaos, and that nobody but God Almighty could finish it."

But that was just the sort of challenge that appealed to Sarah. For the next three years she personally directed every phase of the building—slashing wages, reviewing the books with the energy of a certified public accountant, and turning up many an example of extravagance and inefficiency. Both Duke and Duchess, who were now vastly wealthy, clung to money as lovingly as they had when they were penniless young courtiers. The Duke, ordering a canopy under which to sign a peace treaty, showed his characteristic thrift: "Pray take care to have it made so that it may serve for part of a bed when I have done with it here." Unfortunately, the peace negotiations failed, and the canopy was never made. And the Duchess, at the same time that she writes, with a show of feminine helplessness, "It is so difficult for a Woman to get the better of so many people in the profession of cheating," is arranging with the British ambassador to Venice to bring her some cut velvet in his personal luggage so that she might evade the duty.

By the end of the summer of 1719, the private apartments were finished and furnished; without fanfare, wanting only peace and quiet, the old Duke moved in. For two summers he was able to enjoy his monument, though the peaceful sounds of the country were still interrupted by hammering. He died in June 1722, not at Blenheim, as he surely would have preferred, but at one of his wife's favorite houses, Windsor Lodge. In his will he left Sarah £50,000 for the express purpose of finishing Blenheim. And this she faithfully did, despite a number of lawsuits from the creditors of Blenheim, most of which she lost. (Vanbrugh produced the Lord Treasurer's warrant of 1705, naming Marlborough as builder of Blenheim, and on the strength of it won a percentage of what was owing to him.) Such was Sarah's thrift that she finished the palace for £25,000 instead of £50,000. At her own expense she put up in the park a Column of Victory, surmounted by a seven-ton lead statue of Marlborough, and a triumphal arch to form the main gateway to the grounds. She also added to the Long Library a handsome marble statue of Queen Anne. "I have a real satisfaction in showing this respect to her," she said, "because her kindness to me was real. And what happened afterwards was compassed by the contrivance of such as are in power now." Her last duty was to finish the chapel and bury there the body of her husband, which had temporarily reposed in Westminster. She and her ducal descendants were also to be buried here, beneath an immense marble memorial. It is typical of Sarah's uninhibited pride that the pews in the chapel face this sumptuous grave, while the altar and pulpit, very plain, are off to one side.

Acquitted of her duty in finishing Blenheim, Sarah rarely returned there; she eventually owned thirty estates and preferred any one of them to Blenheim. The Marlborough title passed to Henrietta Churchill, the eldest Marlborough daughter. She died before her mother (who lived to be eighty-four), and the Dukedom went to Charles Spencer, a son of the Marlboroughs' second daughter, Anne. This Duke lived at Blenheim for fifteen years, content to enjoy the house and gardens as he found them; but his son George, Fourth Duke, a man of fashion, culture, and extravagance, found Blenheim out-of-date and set out to modernize it. Under his direction, the landscape architect Lancelot ("Capability") Brown wiped out the parterres, the lime walks, the topiary, the fountains—all Henry Wise's herculean efforts—and substituted grass. He made a lake where the canals and islands had been and flooded the lower rooms of the Grand Bridge—an alteration that remains to this day and which critics have generally agreed complements the imposing grandeur of bridge, palace, and landscape.

Each duke added paintings, furniture, books, and *objets d'art,* usually in the best taste of his age, and subtracted substantially from the family fortunes. And each duke, his duchess, and his children added also to a pattern of formality and tradition as rigid as that of any royal family. A Duke of Marlborough was supposed to live ducally, but also preserve Blenheim intact for succeeding generations. Too much emphasis on ducal living led the Seventh Duke, in the 1880s, to sell a palace treasure, the Sunderland Library, one of the finest rare-book collections in England; the Eighth Duke sold a portrait of Charles I by Van Dyck and Raphael's "Ansidei Madonna." The gardens grew shabby, the leaden Marlborough atop the Column of Victory tipped eleven inches out of alignment. Nevertheless, inside the palace, the ducal family and their noble friends and relatives lived their rank-and-tradition-regulated daily routine—sleeping and dining amid acres of chilly gilt, dressing in dark closets, and prospecting down long corridors to find each other, while housemaids made endless rounds with hot-water jugs and coal scuttles.

But it was time for a major replenishment of the family bank account. The Eighth Duke married, as his second wife, a wealthy American widow, Lilian Warren, and began replanting the gardens; his son, succeeding to the title in 1892, married Consuelo Vanderbilt, whereupon central heating and plumbing invaded the boulder-thick walls. The Bernini fountain was restored, some of the state rooms refurbished (a job that took twenty decorators from Paris six months to finish), the Marlborough statue atop the Column of Victory was put straight—in short, Blenheim was brought back to splendor. The Ninth Duke and the Vanderbilt fortune will probably be remembered longest for the elaborate water-terrace gardens, designed by the French landscape architect Duchêne, which now lie in place of Wise's formal parterres and Capability Brown's grass.

So Blenheim Palace survives and might be classified as one more of the Duke's great victories. Sir Winston Churchill put it this way: "Remembrance may be preserved to remote posterity by piling great stones on one another, and engraving deep inscriptions on them. But fame is not to be so easily captured. Blenheim cost [Marlborough] dear. It weakened him in his relations with hostile Ministers. It exposed him to mockery and malice. The liability for its expense was turned as a weapon against him. In after-years he was forced into unsuccessful litigation with the Crown. In his will he had to leave £50,000 to complete work otherwise derelict. Indeed, his happiness lost much, and his fame gained nothing, by the building of Blenheim. However, Blenheim stands, and [he] would probably regard it as having fulfilled its purpose if he returned to earth at this day."

"A Cluster of Soap Bubbles"
The Alhambra

OF A MAN WITH A SAD AND PENSIVE AIR, NORTH AFRICAN ARABS say, "He is thinking of Granada." The Arabs lost Granada in the year that Columbus discovered America, but still, so it is said, there are Moslem families in North Africa who keep two door keys, one of which is five centuries old and was made for a lock far away across the Strait of Gibraltar. The last Arab ruler of Granada, Mohammed XI—or Boabdil, as he is known in European annals— was not even allowed to keep his keys; that is to say, the keys of his palace, the Alhambra. On January 2, 1492, he turned them over to his conquerors, King Ferdinand and Queen Isabella, and left by way of a southward mountain road, pausing, for one tear-dimmed look backward, at a point that has ever since been called "The Last Sigh of the Moor." Boabdil's people called him "the poor devil," a name that reveals a certain sympathy for a man whose lost palace compared closely with the Koran's description of paradise. A medieval Arab writer once remarked that the Alhambra was too much like paradise and that, therefore, Allah had been obliged to curse it. The curse was that of continual internecine quarreling and bloodshed, and these things eventually brought about the downfall of the dynasty that built it.

During the two and a half centuries of its heyday as the residence of the Nasrid kings of Granada, the Alhambra was without doubt the most elegant, sophisticated, and beautiful dwelling in all the Western world. Writers who have tried to describe it have nearly always lapsed into hyperbole. For example, "Something voluptuous, religious, warlike seemed to emanate from this magnificent edifice," said Chateaubriand in a silly story called "The Adventures of the Last Abencerrage"; "a kind of cloister of love, a mysterious retreat where the Moorish kings tasted all the pleasures and forgot all the duties of life." And Washington Irving: "Every-

A ceiling painting thought to portray one of the sultans of the Nasrid dynasty.

thing invites to that indolent repose, the bliss of southern climes; and while the half-shut eye looks out from shaded balconies upon the glittering landscape, the ear is lulled by the rustling of groves and the murmur of running streams."

But to get down to earth, the name "Alhambra" refers to a complex of buildings on top of a hill, called the Sabika, that rises like an acropolis in the midst of the city of Granada. This complex has three distinct components. First, a fortress, the Alcazaba, which predates the rest, its oldest tower having been built in the ninth century. The rubble at its base includes a piece of a votive altar ("The grateful Valens to his most indulgent wife, Cornelia"), showing that the Romans were there, too. Second, a servants' area, now largely torn down; and, third, a residence. This residence, which is the beautiful part of the Alhambra, is itself divided according to customary palace planning in the Near East. The main outer gate is called the Gate of Justice, the area in front of palace gates being the traditional seat of justice among the Moslems. Next comes the throne room and other halls and courtyards for official entertaining, and then the king's private quarters and the harem, with windows overlooking the sheerest descent of the hill.

In the near distance, poised on a higher hilltop, is a summer pleasure dome, the Generalife; and, on the horizon, the splendid summits of the Sierra Nevada. The views from the Alhambra must be counted as part of its glory: mountains in one direction, and elsewhere a rich plain that is flowery in spring, green in summer, and golden in fall and winter. The white villas dotted here and there reminded a medieval Arab poet of "Oriental pearls set in a cup of emerald." Théophile Gautier, who lived for several months in Granada in the 1840s, wrote, describing a sunset: "The mountains sparkle like vast heaps of rubies, topazes, and carbuncles; the spaces between are filled with a golden dust, and if, as often occurs in summer, the peasants are burning straw in the plain, the wisps of smoke which slowly rise heavenward are colored by the rays of the setting sun with exquisite tints."

The assets of Granada's site were probably first recognized by cave men, and when the Romans arrived in Andalusia, in the third century B.C., they found a well-inhabited country that had been settled first by Ibero-Celts and then by Carthaginians. In due course, Roman colonists were succeeded by Visigoths. Then, early in the eighth century, came violent new conquerors, the Arabs, and with them that indigenous North African people, the Berbers, whom the Arabs had converted to Islam and who had become more fanatical evangelists than the Arabs themselves.

Visigothic society in Spain was corrupt and chaotic, consisting of a few rich landowners and hordes of discontented serfs. About

RIGHT: View from the Alcazaba fort of the Jardin de
Machuca, and the west side of
the Alcazar with the great
tower or Torre de Comares.
BELOW: General view of the
Alhambra.

Martin Hurlimann

H. Armstrong Roberts

a third of the Andalusian population was Jewish, descendants of families dispersed from Jerusalem in the days of Hadrian (himself an Andalusian). The Jews preferred the more tolerant and sophisticated rule of the Arabs to that of the cloddish Visigoths and gladly abetted the new arrivals. On the site of modern Granada there was a Jewish town called Garnatha Alyehud, and the name "Granada" is thought to derive from this.

The people from the deserts of North Africa and the Near East were delighted by the green, watery country in which they now found themselves and urged their relatives at home to join them. In successive waves they came, the flood tide reaching as far north as Poitiers, in southern France, where it was finally turned back by Charles Martel in 732. The Arabs, or Moors, to use the usual term for North Africans in Spain, held power in the Spanish peninsula for nearly eight centuries (the Roman Empire was far less durable). But for most of that time they ruled only over the south, al-Andalus, and made it the richest and most intellectual region in Europe. Toward the end of the eleventh century a Berber potentate who had been invited to Spain by the caliph of Seville to help in the wars against the Christians turned on the caliph and captured Granada and other important cities. In 1238 an independent Arab leader named Mohammed al-Ahmar (Mohammed "the Red") took Granada from the Berbers. He founded his own line of rulers, the Nasrid dynasty. Twenty-eight kings and two and a half centuries later, this dynasty came to an end with the hapless Boabdil.

It was al-Ahmar who began to build the Alhambra. The name "Alhambra" is thought to derive from the Arabic *kala hamra* (red castle), and refers either to its builder's nickname or to the reddish color of its bricks. A more poetic theory is that the flickering of torchlight during night construction work gave rise to the name "the Red." Most of what we see today was the work of two of al-Ahmar's descendants, Yusuf I and his son Mohammed V, who ruled in the fourteenth century. The palace has no architectural unity, but consists of a series of halls and courtyards that were built as they were needed or wanted. Each is inward-turning, self-absorbed, and self-sufficient. The views that so inspire the modern visitor's admiration were in Moorish days chiefly left to the sentries—or, perhaps (one's imagination runs wild in a place like this), to captured Christian maidens scanning the horizon for signs of rescuing armies. The ruler and his courtiers liked to keep aloof from the outside world, secluded in their exquisitely proportioned courtyards and chambers. "Hail, thou, welcome, joyful fabric," cries an Arab poet, addressing the Alhambra. "All men are in awe of thy filigreed tissue, like the tissue of Spring when the rain falls."

46

To Gautier, who was allowed to live in the palace for a few days, the walls looked like "plaster embroidery," and the delicate honeycomb moldings like "a cluster of soap bubbles which children blow with a straw," and, in fact, much of the Alhambra is not a great deal more substantial than that, being made of nothing more enduring than stucco on top of a reed scaffolding. These Moorish sojourners in an ever-encroaching hostile land did not build for the future and would no doubt be astonished to find that their playful fancies have outlasted parts of the solid and seemingly unbudgeable fortress that shares the same hill. For the Alhambra's preservation we have to thank the Catholic sovereigns of Spain, most of whom kept it in decent repair. Charles V was the only one who actively disliked the place ("the ugly abomination of the Moors," he called it); and he tore down part of it to make room for a grandiose Renaissance palace for himself. This was never finished, and stands there today, forlorn and roofless. It is a monument to poor judgment—blameless in its way, but totally out-of-place, like a dinner guest who has come in black tie when the invitation said fancy dress.

The Moors disapproved of representational art, and the Alhambra is chiefly adorned with geometric designs in a wealth of variation. The Hall of the Kings has painted ceilings that show scenes of court life, and the Patio de los Leones takes its name from twelve stone lions guarding its central fountain—but these heresies were the results of frivolous Christian influences. The lions are believed to have been the work of Christian captives, while the ceilings have been ascribed by some to a Christian artist of the fourteenth century. Inscriptions in Arabic or Kufic characters are integral with the stucco decoration. To those of us who cannot read them, they look merely decorative, but a student of the language finds that they are either verses from the Koran or poems in praise of the architecture and the sultans.

Look upon this wonderful cupola, at sight of whose perfection all other domes must pale and disappear./To which the Constellation of the Twins extends the hand of salutation; and, for communion, the Full Moon deserts her station in heavens.

I am the garden, and every morn am I revealed in new beauty. Observe attentively how I am adorned, and thou wilt reap the benefit of a commentary on decoration.

Interspersed with all these high-flying sentiments is the grave reminder, repeated on every wall, "Only God is Conqueror,"

OVERLEAF: The Court of Lions.

"How poor and wretched our lives would be if our hopes were not so high and great," said the first Nasrid king, al-Ahmar. The world in which he built his pleasure dome was dark and menacing. A realist, al-Ahmar bought peace for his kingdom by going in person to the Christian king of Castile, Ferdinand III, and becoming his vassal, even though this meant providing troops to fight King Ferdinand's Moslem enemies. In spite of the basic mortal enmity between Christian and Moor in Spain, considerable intercourse existed. Al-Ahmar's subjects adopted certain Christian styles of dress and of arms, and the Christians provided an enthusiastic market for the crafts of Granada, such as magnificent textiles, carpets, tooled leather, carved ivory, inlaid woods, and wrought metals. Sometimes there were even voluntary marriages between Christians and Moslems, including arranged royal matches.

"The women of Granada," says Ibn al-Khatib, a fourteenth-century chronicler, "are graceful, elegant, and svelte; it is rare to find one who is ill-proportioned. They are neat, take great pains to arrange their long hair . . . Their charms are highlighted by their graceful manners, exquisite discretion and delightful conversation. It is regrettable, however, that we are reaching a moment in which the women of Granada are carrying the magnificence of their attire and adornment to the brink of fantasy." Every generation has its scolds and misanthropes, particularly on the subject of women's dress; nevertheless, there was probably an air of reckless abandon about Granadine society, for it was a doomed one and realized it. Al-Ahmar used his dearly bought peace to improve the prosperity of his country, and it became so rich that it was reputed to have discovered the secret of turning base metal into gold. Neighboring Christians, eying its rich industries and fruitful countryside, became more zealous than ever in their efforts to save its infidel soul.

Al-Ahmar lived to be seventy-nine, and left a thriving kingdom. Of his twenty successors, the most distinguished was Yusuf I (1333–1354), a cultured and chivalrous king who ruled his subjects wisely, fended off the Christians, and established the University of Granada, over whose gates he wrote, "The world is supported by four things only: the learning of the wise, the justice of the great, the prayers of the righteous and the valor of the brave." Yusuf also found time to build the most beautiful parts of the Alhambra: notably, the Hall of the Ambassadors, and the Hall of the Two Sisters. Expert engineering, begun by al-Ahmar, brought an abundance of water to the heights of the Alhambra, and the murmuring of fountains mingled delightfully with the songs of birds and the rustling of foliage. Perhaps it was this continuity of sound, coupled with the repetitious style of decoration, that gave the palace its strange feeling of timelessness. As in the Koran's paradise, there were never any abrupt transitions; one lived there shut off from the world, the light filtering in through lattices and stained glass or falling obliquely into courtyards. Each room, each court, with its airy and fragile arches, was an end in itself. And, in a hundred variations of wording, the poetical inscriptions said, in effect, "This is perfection; why seek further?" No wonder that a worldly and pragmatic soul like Charles V could see no point in the Alhambra.

But, despite its languid and sensuous atmosphere, the palace was anything but tranquil. There were twenty-one rulers in 254 years, and since both al-Ahmar and Yusuf I had comfortably long reigns of forty-one and twenty-one years respectively, it is plain that many of the other monarchs had curiously short reigns. These medieval Moors, who loved poetry and learning, who studied Aristotle and Euclid, whose knowledge of geography influenced Columbus, and whose advances in medicine laid the foundations of surgery in Europe, were nevertheless often bloodthirsty, cruel, and vicious. Whether they were more so than their Christian brethren of the same period it is hard to say, but theirs was a civilization literally backed into a corner, and perhaps that gave them less time for the amenities. An often-told story about the Alhambra concerns the wholesale murder of thirty-six young men of a noble Granadine family, the Abencerrages, whom the king suspected of treason and therefore summoned, one by one, to be beheaded. (The guides who show tourists the Hall of Abencerrages point out, as evidence, reddish stains on the marble fountain.) Only one Abencerrage was warned and managed to escape.

The struggles of the Nasrid kings and their relatives are too confusing and too obscure to retell here. It is pleasanter to reflect that, in spite of the most lethal quarrels, there was also a great deal of singing, dancing, and partying in these sequestered courts; also, a great deal of *tarab*. *Tarab* is a kind of physical reaction to pleasures of the mind and spirit—thus, the recitation of a particularly delightful poem might cause the listeners to faint, foam at the mouth, tear their clothes, or beat their heads against the wall. A modern Spanish writer, Emilio García Gómez, has commented, "The loss of this capacity for great physical emotion—even in its less violent forms—seems to me to show a present-day lack of sensitivity. If any trace of *tarab* remains, it must be sought at the bullfight or at other sporting events. But no . . . the 'olé of the *canto hondo* is still the *wallah* ('O God!') with which the Arabs cheered every poetic recitation."

Northern Europeans, whose *tarab* is confined to a polite patting of the hands together or perhaps an occasional rusty "bravo" at the opera, are usually embarrassed by demonstrations of emotion. Yet the sensuous South, the home of emotional excess, has always held a strange fascination for them; and over the centuries that followed the defeat and departure of the Moors, the Alhambra became a favorite of travelers, both armchair and actual. After Ferdinand and Isabella took it over from Boabdil, Granada ceased to be a royal capital. The treaty of 1492 was remarkably lenient with the Moors and permitted them to stay in Granada without religious oppression. But this treaty was soon violated. In 1556 the fanatical Philip II ordered the Moors who remained in Andalusia to give up their language, religion, and manner of life. During the next one hundred and fifty years all Moslems were either executed or expelled from Spain—about three million of them—and al-Andalus became the conspicuous exception to the historical fact that wherever Arabs established their civilization they remained. Granada became a Christian city and the Alhambra a little-used summer palace of the Spanish royal family. In the early eighteenth century several rooms were refurbished for the honeymoon of Philip V and his bride, Elizabeth of Parma; but, in the main, the palace drowsed through the centuries, inhabited only by caretakers and their relatives. The relatives proliferated so that the palace was like a little town; but, being there on sufferance of the governor of Granada, they behaved in a circumspect manner, and if they planted cabbages in the royal flower beds, they were careful to leave the roses.

The only war to disturb Granada in the post-Moorish era was Napoleon's Spanish campaign. Fortunately, the Romantic Age was in full flower, and the occupying forces—first the French and then the English—were respectful of antiquity. The French, although they blew up two of the most ancient towers of the fortress when they departed, did some restoration work on some of the more fragile stuccoes; the English, under the Duke of Wellington, planted English elms on the slopes outside the walls, and it is through this charming old wood that the modern tourist ascends to do his sightseeing. (In the days of the Moors the slopes, for defensive reasons, were bare of trees, and were largely given over to a cemetery.)

One spring day in 1829 a well-dressed gentleman tourist, traveling on horseback, arrived before the plains of Granada, as Ferdinand and Isabella and al-Ahmar and the Visigoths, Romans, Carthaginians, and Ibero-Celts had arrived before him. "The day was without a cloud. The heat of the sun was tempered by cool breezes from the mountains . . . In the distance was romantic Granada surmounted by the ruddy towers of the Alhambra, while far above it the snowy summits of the Sierra Nevada shone like silver." Like his predecessors, Washington Irving decided to stay here as

Twin windows in the Hall of the Two Sisters, or Sala de las Dos Hermanas, in which Arabic calligraphic symbols are used as decoration.

long as possible. Possessed of a charming personality and polished manners, as well as of the right letters of introduction, he was invited by the governor to make himself at home in the Alhambra. And there he stayed for several months. "My meals are made wherever caprice dictates," he wrote, "sometimes in one of the Moorish halls, sometimes under the arcades of the Court of Lions, surrounded by flowers and fountains." One night he scared himself half to death by sleeping in the long-empty apartments of Elizabeth of Parma, where he heard "stifled shrieks and inarticulate ravings." These turned out to be the cries of an insane relative of the concierge. And one sunny afternoon, while strolling about the ramparts, he came upon a peasant "maneuvering two or three fishing rods, as though he were angling for the stars." He was catching swallows and martlets, "with hooks baited with flies."

The book that Irving wrote about his experiences, *Tales of the Alhambra*, was on every nineteenth-century parlor table, and many other eminent writers made Granada a point of pilgrimage and of literary effusion. Thus, the Alhambra entered its third and final phase: a symbol of a world too beautiful and romantic to exist, but ah! if it only could! A replica of the Court of Lions was a feature of the Crystal Palace Exhibition of 1851; businessmen adorned the drab walls of their offices with "The Court of the Myrtles," "The Garden of Lindaraja," and so on, painstakingly rendered in steel engravings; the Alhambra influence erupted in all sorts of unexpected places—for example, in Cincinnati, where an exotic-looking shop called Trollope's Bazaar (belonging to the famous, America-hating Mrs. Trollope) was a careful imitation of Alhambra architecture. But, as one nineteenth-century English traveler pointed out, the Alhambra was "peculiar to its society," and could be neither imitated nor rivaled.

And now the days when a tourist could set up housekeeping there are over; now you can only trail meekly through on a guided tour, without benefit of moonlight, nightingales, or even "stifled shrieks and inarticulate ravings." You cannot fish, either for stars or swallows, from the ramparts, but if the crowd is not too great, you may be allowed to pause there for a moment and look at the Sierra Nevada. It still shines like silver, just as it did for Washington Irving and for al-Ahmar.

The Emperor's Folly
Hadrian's Villa

"UNDER HIS REIGN, THE EMPIRE FLOURISHED IN PEACE AND prosperity," says Gibbon of the Emperor Hadrian. "He encouraged the arts, reformed the laws, asserted military discipline, and visited all his provinces in person. His vast and active genius was equally suited to the most enlarged views and the minute details of civil policy. But the ruling passions of his soul were curiosity and vanity."

Hadrian has been dead for more than eighteen hundred years, and nearly all the achievements of his "vast and active genius" are void and forgotten. But evidence of the passions that ruled him—boundless curiosity and unembarrassed vanity—still survives, particularly among the ruins of the most sumptuous, least cozy, most odd and remarkable country seat ever built: Hadrian's Villa at Tivoli, outside Rome.

Not a great deal is known about Hadrian's personality. He wrote an autobiography but it is lost, and his only ancient biographers lived in the second and fourth centuries, some time after his death. His public and military accomplishments can be pieced together from contemporary letters, coins, and inscriptions, but to find out what he was like as a man is much more difficult. This amazing villa of his, which he built for his own personal delight and solace, is the closest thing we have to a memoir—even though in its very ruined state it makes enigmatic and abstract reading.

If you approach Hadrian's Villa along the route prescribed for tourists, you encounter, first of all, an enormous masonry wall. Its dimensions are so imposing—about twenty-eight feet high and more than seven hundred feet long—as to raise your hopes that these ruins will not be very ruined. But after you have passed through a gate, you perceive that the wall is just standing there by itself, like an upsided ruler, and that on the other side of it is simply a very big, rectangular, grassy space containing a pond. There are various ruins in the distance, but here there is not a statue, not a column, not so much as a stone-on-stone. If you consult a guidebook, you find yourself called upon to imagine that this huge rectangle is enclosed by three more walls, that these walls, plus many marble columns, are the supports for splendidly painted porticoes, that the grassy space is enriched by flowers, statues, and fountains, and that here and there the courtiers of Hadrian are strolling or marching about getting up an appetite for lunch.

This is only the beginning of a considerable job of imagining. Ahead, spread out on the rolling plain that skirts the Sabine hills, lie one hundred and fifty acres of thoroughly ruined ruins. Much more is still to be excavated, for it is known that when Hadrian died, in A.D. 138, his Villa covered more than seven square miles, three-fourths the area of Rome itself. This was not a villa in the modern sense, but a collection of building complexes: an out-of-the-ordinary town, rich in splendidly decorated piazzas, domed halls, and belvederes, and poor in the usual amenities, such as bedrooms, kitchens, and nurseries. The place has been called the Versailles of the Caesars, but Versailles, for all its glitter and show, was essentially a dwelling; while the Villa seems an abstraction, an *assemblage*.

Hadrian was, as Tertullian said of him, *"omnium curiositatum explorator"*; as a student in Greece, a soldier in Dacia, a governor in Asia Minor, and a Roman emperor traveling to every corner of his empire, he was a tireless collector of beautiful things, and he needed a place to put all the treasures, and copies of treasures, that he brought home with him. If he could have collected the Acropolis and the pyramids, one feels he would have done so. His particular passion was architecture. As an ordinary man putters in his tool shop, Hadrian, on the plains of Tibur, puttered with life-sized domes and vaults and peristyles, sometimes copying, more often improvising, but always building for building's sake and for the sake of housing statues and paintings.

Hadrian began traveling and sight-seeing at an early age. Born in A.D. 76 in Andalusia, a Roman province, where his family were colonists, he went to Rome at the age of ten, on the death of his father, and was educated there under the supervision of his two guardians, one of whom was Trajan, at that time an important military commander. Hadrian's tutors were Greek, and they inspired him with a lifelong love for Greek culture; his schoolmates

Roman portrait bust of Hadrian, in marble, from the Villa Montalto in Rome.

Edwin Smith (from *Art Treasures of the British Museum*, Thames and Hudson Ltd.)

called him "the Greekling." When he grew up, Athens, not Rome, was his favorite city, and most of his Villa is of Greek derivation.

At fifteen Hadrian returned to Spain, and at nineteen began his long public career by serving as a tribune at the particular section of the Roman frontier that is now Budapest. Three years later, in A.D. 98, Trajan succeeded Nerva as emperor, and in A.D. 100 Hadrian was married to Sabina, Trajan's great-niece and nearest living relative. It was generally assumed that Hadrian would succeed Trajan, but Trajan lived seventeen more years, and not until he was on his deathbed did he make Hadrian his official adopted son and heir.

Childless and unhappily married, Hadrian put all his tremendous energies into work and continual activity. Until he was well into his fifties—an old man, by Roman standards—he went on traveling, often marching great distances and sleeping in the open. From Scotland to the Euphrates, from the Rhine to the deserts of North Africa, everywhere he went he collected not only objects but ideas. And one can imagine that during this time he amused himself by planning the great Villa that was to be an end-of-the-road for all this traveling and collecting. In the year 131 his health began to fail, and from then until his death in 138 Hadrian stayed at home and concentrated on his vast toy.

Such a forgathering of the world's most talented craftsmen and artists and such an amassment of precious materials has rarely been seen in the world before or since. Whole porphyry columns came by galley from Egypt, and, from the quarries of North Africa, great slabs of serpentine, *giallo antico*, and alabaster. It was quite impossible for Hadrian to be too lavish with himself; the notion that a sovereign could be criticized for not watching expenses had not yet occurred to anyone.

Hadrian did not die at the Villa. Even in the last stages of illness he was restless, and he died while on a short trip to Baiae, on the Bay of Naples. But if he called any place home, it was surely the great Villa at Tibur. Perhaps it was too distinctively his ever to seem homelike to anyone else, for his successors do not appear to have spent much time there.

In the third century Queen Zenobia is said to have been held a prisoner there. In the sixth century conquering Goths used the Villa as a fortress. Subsequent barbaric devastations alternated with long periods when the Villa was a Sleeping Beauty's castle, left to the vandalism of weeds and vines. People forgot what it was. The peasants of the neighborhood supposed that it had been a Roman town, and when they needed building stones or ornaments for the new, nearby town of Tivoli, they got them from there. In 1538 Cardinal Ippolito d'Este began to build the Villa d'Este at Tivoli.

The architect, a Neapolitan named Ligorio, took much inspiration and a good deal of adornment from the ancient Villa for the new one.

In 1461 Pope Pius II, paying the ruins a visit, wrote that "the sublime and vast vaults" remained. "Time has marred everything," he went on. "The walls once covered with embroidered tapestries and hangings threaded with gold are now clothed with ivy. Briers and brambles have sprung up where purple-robed tribunes sat and queens' chambers are the lairs of serpents. So fleeting are mortal things!" But it was not only time that marred things at Hadrian's Villa. Although the barbarians had taken away what was easily portable, such as candelabra, plates, and jewels, and the citizens of Tivoli had managed to move a few larger items, it was left to the popes, cardinals, and princes of the Baroque Age to abscond with whole mosaics, inlaid marble floors, columns, capitals, and statues.

Statues of Antinoüs, Hadrian's favorite, must have been numbered in dozens, judging by the quantity now in the museums of Europe. Bernini, in his memoirs, mentioned that one such statue, taken from the Villa and placed in the Vatican, was a great help to him in studying the art of sculpture.

By the eighteenth century, when ruins and archaeology became a fashionable intellectual interest and English noblemen made the Villa a scheduled stop on the Grand Tour, nearly everything beautiful that had been in sight had been carted away. Piranesi's engravings show parts of the Villa looking just about as they do now, except much weedier. The stucco ceilings, like those at Pompeii, inspired the British architect Robert Adam, who went home to adorn the great houses of England with the delicate stucco designs of the Romans. Here and there at the Villa are bits and pieces of ceilings. They seem so typically Adam and eighteenth-century that it gives one a shock to realize that they are about fifteen hundred years older.

During the eighteenth century two families who had farms in the area turned archaeology into a paying business. The Fede family, whose house was more or less on top of a Temple of Venus, sold what they excavated to wealthy Romans: for example, sixteen marble columns and a colossal Antinoüs now in the Vatican, and two marble gladiators that eventually found their way into the hands of a king of Poland. The Bulgarini family, owners of a large part of the ruins, sold excavation rights until legally restrained from doing so late in the nineteenth century. They kept businesslike records of everything that was looted, and these records have been a great help to modern archaeologists.

During this time of enthusiastic but irresponsible interest, a lot of conclusions were jumped to, and various parts of the Villa were given identifications that, though wrong, have stuck. The official guidebook goes on using these labels, prefixing them with "so-called" and adding to the general confusion. Thus, the vast rectangle at the entrance gate is "the so-called Pecile." "Pecile" is a word derived from the Greek *stoa poikile*, or painted portico. It was thought that this area was a copy of the *Stoa Poikile* in Athens. Subsequently it has been pointed out that the Athenian painted portico was of quite a different shape and size and that Hadrian was not attempting to reproduce it, though he may have been inspired by it. The so-called Pecile appears as flat ground, but under its southwest end is a three-storied honeycomb of small rooms, the "so-called Hundred Rooms" (actually there are a hundred and sixty). These were storerooms, servants' rooms, and guards' rooms, and were—and still are—connected by a network of underground passageways that traveled all over the Villa. The lower orders at the Villa were lower orders quite literally—living their lives in their dank dormitories or padding back and forth through these service tunnels, emerging sometimes into the glitter and sunshine of some sumptuous apartment to deliver a cooling drink or wield a peacock fan.

These humid, dark "Hundred Rooms" are just the right sort of place for growing mushrooms, and a few years ago the incumbent Supervisor of the Ruins, anxious to supplement his modest civil-service salary, started a private business of renting them out to mushroom growers. It was not until some archaeologists discovered that the tenants were making structural changes that the matter came to public attention and both mushroom-growers and supervisor were removed from the premises. The same enterprising public servant allowed a camping site to be established directly next to the Villa, so the gentle country sounds that have always been there—songs of birds, goat bells, the braying of donkeys—are now supplemented and sometimes drowned out by the campers' radios.

In Hadrian's day the predominant sound was that of splashing water. No part of the Villa was without one or several fountains, and after the water had performed its assigned acrobatics, the Emperor's practical engineers caused it to flow through the latrines and thence away through sewers. One part of the Villa, shaped like a hippodrome and known since Cardinal d'Este's time as "the Stadium," was carefully excavated a few years ago and found to have been a garden, enhanced by many fountains and pools. At one end a tremendous fountain, similar to the Fountain of Trevi, cascaded down a semicircular bank of steps that looks very much like seats in a stadium. The fountain basins bear traces of blue paint, which must have made the water as blue as a Hollywood pool.

The plaster model at the entrance to the villa today, recording the fact that many celebrated places in Roman provinces inspired the villa's design.

Next door to this garden is an area known as the Fishpond Quadriportico. Here, a large pond—possibly it was a swimming pool—was enclosed by a quadriportico built on two levels. The upper level was a roofed colonnade and the lower, below ground level but lit by high-up windows, was a cool and airy tunnel for walking on hot days. This architectural caprice, known as a cryptoportico, was a favorite with Hadrian. Psychologists, attempting to analyze the Emperor across the centuries, have said that his love of shadowy places, of the interplay of light and shade, and of the inconstant constancy of running water, indicates a tendency to restlessness, ambivalence, even schizophrenia. They point out also that the Villa is schizophrenically planned: it has no harmony as a whole but is divided into aesthetically unrelated complexes. Each building is oriented to sun and view rather than to its neighbors.

If certain aspects of the Villa seem to indicate that Hadrian was eccentric, others are monuments to his genius. For example, a certain room in the "Bath Complex" is regarded as one of the wonders of ancient architecture: its walls form an octagon, with alternately straight and convex sides, and its ceiling once soared dizzily for nine free-flying yards—a distance never achieved before

61

and rarely since. Now, only a skeletal remnant of the vaults remains, and where the bathers used to congregate, great chunks of fallen masonry lie like burned-out meteorites.

One of the most splendid parts of the Villa, known as "Canopus," has been thoroughly excavated only in the past ten years. All evidence agrees that here Hadrian set out to represent Canopus, a sanctuary of the Egyptian god Serapis, which lay at the head of a canal on the Nile, near Alexandria. It was a place the Emperor must have remembered with particular fondness and poignancy, having visited it in the company of his beloved Antinoüs, who drowned shortly afterward. Hadrian represented the canal by digging a basin, about 390 feet long, in the hollow of a small valley, and filling it with water. For many hundreds of years this basin was filled in and grown over, but recent excavations have cleared it and brought up a fine haul of statues that once stood at the water's brink: four caryatids, copies of those on the Acropolis in Athens; two heroic-sized Sileni, with baskets on their heads; reclining figures representing the river Nile and the river Tiber; a life-sized crocodile, carved in *cipollino*, a marble whose green mottling makes it the ideal medium in which to sculpt crocodiles; copies of famous works by Phidias and Polyclitus; and much more.

The narrow valley that contains the water basin of Canopus rises steeply on two sides and at one end, and at this end Hadrian built an amazingly elaborate nymphaeum, or fountain building. What we see of it today is an enormous, ruined half-dome, or hemicycle, beneath which a honeycomb of odd corridors and niches retreat into the hillside. In Hadrian's day an aqueduct brought water to a distribution tank at the highest point in this building, whence it flowed through corridors, cascaded down walls, splashed into basins, spurted from niches, and ended by joining the large, placid pool of Canopus. At the lower reaches of this Niagara, sheltered by the outer rim of the half-dome, was an open-air dining room, a semicircle of stone couches where the Roman elite might recline and, while gorging themselves, admire the statues and columns reflected in the pool, the glittering domes of the Villa and, beyond, the same gentle hills and limpid sunset we see today. There must have been a lot of random spray, but perhaps on a summer evening this would have felt refreshing.

Across yet unexcavated fields to the right and at the back of the great nymphaeum are two more self-oriented parts of the Villa. The "so-called Tower of Roccabruna" is—or, rather, was—a three-storied square building with a ramp inside it and a belvedere at the top. Hadrian's purpose in building it, as well as the significance of the medieval name "Roccabruna," is lost in time. (One suspects that Hadrian simply wanted to see what a three-storied square building with a ramp inside it and a belvedere on top would look like.)

On the highest point of ground in the entire Villa is the "so-called Academy"—*not* an academy, but modeled architecturally on the Academy at Athens. It was perhaps built for the Emperor to live in during very hot weather, when the sheltered slope below was not airy enough. One can imagine him being carried in a litter to this expensively adorned hilltop for a breath of humble fresh air. Some of the finest of the Villa's works of art were found at the "Academy," including the famous mosaic showing two doves on the rim of a vase, which, since 1745, has been in the Capitoline Museum. The Academy complex includes, besides the usual water-works and courtyards, a well-preserved theater. No fewer than three theaters have been found at the Villa, but no stadium or arena, from which we may be safe in assuming that chariot races, gladia-torial fights, and the public disposal of Christians were not among the Emperor's preferred diversions. Not that he did not believe in the extermination of Christians—at the celebrations marking the opening of the Villa, a Christian woman and her seven sons were put to death. But, on the whole, human-blood sports were not in Hadrian's line. One feels that they did not shock him, they merely bored him—although not as much as they bored his adoptive grandson, Marcus Aurelius, who used to take a book along when-ever duty called him to the Colosseum.

Hadrian had his own recherché forms of amusement, and one of these, as has already been noted, was walking about in crypto-porticoes. Near the "Academy" he built one that is over half a mile long and is intended to represent the Inferi, the Roman underworld. It is roughly trapezoidal in shape, so that one could walk in it without turning back and return to the starting point. It was lit, at intervals of about thirty-six feet, by openings that gave a worm's or lost soul's view of the sunny world above. More rabbit warrens connected it to the "Academy," and to the "so-called Piazza d'Oro."

The Piazza d'Oro is the largest peristyle of the Villa and was given that name by Ligorio, the architect of the Villa d'Este, who was particularly pleased by the amount of loot he found there. It occupies the highest part of a long slope, which is terraced in a series of four large peristyles, each with rooms grouped around it. These rooms, in the opinion of most archaeologists, were the private apart-ments of Hadrian and those nearest him. On the north side of the piazza is an octagonal vestibule with a cupola that has eight concave sides—a highly original scheme and an important source of inspira-tion to baroque architects. On the south side of the piazza is a one-fourth-scale replica of the Pantheon.

The scale of these ruined courtyards and grand buildings suggests anything but a private place to live. In fact, there is only one corner of the entire Villa that looks as if it were built for privacy, and that is the extraordinary moated island that archaeologists are now calling the Island Nymphaeum. In the lee of the slope where the grand peristyles overlook the Vale of Tempe, a twenty-foot circular wall encloses a circular colonnade; the colonnade borders a circular moat about ten feet wide, and in the middle of the moat is a circular island about eighty-two feet in diameter. The dates on the bricks, corresponding to A.D. 123, reveal that this was one of the first constructions at the Villa. Perhaps it was something that the Emperor, who led a very public life, had especially longed for.

The moat was crossed by two drawbridges which, it is thought, were raised when the Emperor wanted to be alone, or perhaps when he and his intimates wanted to swim around the island. The bridges were certainly there for reasons of privacy rather than safety, for a child could have stormed this delicate marble fortress. What each small room was used for can only be conjectured: for sleeping, for reading, for making love, for directing the Roman Empire. But certainly this was a sanctum sanctorum, and you feel,

Each of the ten guest rooms contained three beds set in alcoves. The floors were patterned with mosaics, and light was admitted through a skylight.

Fototeca Unione, Rom

as you invade it, that had you been alive in Hadrian's day, you would never have got near the place and even now are trespassing. Restoration has been carried out as far as possible—and farther, if you listen to some irate archaeologists—through funds made available by the Pirelli Company, manufacturers of tires. It is said that Signor Pirelli was particularly taken with the design of this nymphaeum: it reminded him of a tire.

The fact that Hadrian chose to build on the plain rather than on the exposed and breezier hillside shows that he wanted to enjoy his villa the year round. The moated island is sheltered from wintry winds by its great wall; and nearby is a small, sheltered bath that includes a heliocaminus, or room for sun-bathing. This circular room had five great windows in it, facing south, and the floor was heated. Marble seats, arranged in tiers as in a stadium, are still fairly intact, and if you sit here on a bright winter day, you can feel the sunshine gathering force, warming you just as it warmed the Emperor himself. Here, between timeless sun and timeless stone, the past seems to stir a little. Elsewhere in the Villa you have come much, much too late; but in the sun's terms it is scarcely later at all. Hadrian was here just this morning.

BELOW: Caryatids, Sileni, and a life-size crocodile in green marble adorn the Canopus. OVERLEAF: At the southern end of the Canopus are casts of original statues.

Palace in the Sun
The Grand Palace, Bangkok

"IN THE SOLAR SYSTEM OF SIAM, THE PALACE IS THE SUN," wrote an English diplomat who visited Bangkok in 1894. "When the Palace awakes, everything awakes; when the Palace sleeps, everything sleeps—officialdom, politics, work, duties, pleasures. . . . The foreign element is, in fact, completely outside the real life of Siam . . . To the Palace, therefore, one must speedily find one's way, to see things as they are, or in any sense to know Siam."

In the solar system of modern Thailand this palace is the sun no longer. The present king has moved to newer and more Westernized accommodations; the prime minister and the cabinet members (the real rulers of the country) now have their headquarters on a broad new avenue modeled after the Champs Elysées; and the historic old palace is now part museum, part offices for the bureaucracy, and part haunted house.

In the frantic world of tourism, however, the palace still fulfills a sunlike function. Any visitor to Bangkok who indicates a wish to go sight-seeing is sped immediately to the palace, where, in fierce sun or monsoon rain, he is herded relentlessly from building to building (for this palace consists of a great number of them). Most tourists who fetch up in Bangkok—and there are several hundred thousand a year, conveyed thither by twenty-four airlines—are either on their way around the world or are making a lightning circuit of Southeast Asia, between visits to the tailors and dressmakers of Hong Kong. In either case, they are apt to be dazed by the speed and strangeness of it all; and, probably, they have never before been so hot. To people in this dizzied state, the Grand Palace may seem like a hallucination; they may wonder, afterward, if they really saw such a place.

The approach to the palace is by car through the congested streets of Bangkok. A visitor's first sight of it is a high whitewashed wall from behind which rises a little forest of glittering spires and rooftops. Bangkok is a flat city of low, nondescript buildings, and the sudden view of this thicket of spires is its most impressive sight. Passing through the first gate and leaving his car, the tourist finds himself in a grassy compound about two hundred yards square, with barracks and offices opening onto it; he now perceives that the spires are within a second wall, to the left, but his guide will march him off in another direction, through a double gateway, where he buys a ticket, and into another compound. Before him is the Chakri Palace, completed in 1880, which is saved from looking like a Victorian city hall by a glittering Thai roof. A Thai roof, one of the few original contributions of Thailand to the world of architecture, is in three tiers and slopes steeply, the two lower tiers being less steep than the upper one. The end of each roof ridge is decorated with a sort of finial known as a *chofa*. This suggests an animal's horn; some historians believe that distant, animistic ancestors of the Thai must have mounted the horns of animals on their rooftops to bring good luck. Whatever its origin, the *chofa* has no function now other than an aesthetic one.

Returning toward the glittering spires, the visitor now enters the compound of the Temple of the Emerald Buddha and finds that these spires rise directly from the ground, unlike spires in most countries. To erect one is a way of "acquiring merit." One of the spires in this compound is entirely covered in gold leaf, and others are a mass of bright-colored glass mosaic. In fact, nothing has been left plain; and many Occidentals, brought up on the Cape Cod cottage or on Mies van der Rohe, find the place unnerving.

The Emerald Buddha itself, inside its gilded, mother-of-pearl, painted, carved, and inlaid temple, is a small seated figure, a mere twenty-six inches high, that is said to have been sent from heaven during a thunderstorm in 1436. It is actually not emerald at all, but jasper. Brought to Bangkok at the end of the eighteenth century, it was placed here in the king's own temple at the top of an altar that is sixty feet high. In each of the three Thai seasons of the year—hot, cool, and rainy—the Buddha is dressed in a different costume. The king himself comes to the temple and changes the Buddha's dress.

Compared to other great palaces of the world, this one is not very old. It is, in fact, close to the age of the White House but the similarity ends there. Nothing lasts very long in Thailand; the heat and humidity and the termites are always waiting to attack whatever is put up. But, more or less as we are the same people we were as children, the Grand Palace is the same palace it was in the eighteenth century. The plan is the same: a walled-in compound more than a square mile in area, with the outer part, known as "in front," forming a continuous corridor. This section was designed to include barracks, minor offices, accommodations for white elephants, and the Temple of the Emerald Buddha. Then comes a second high wall, behind which were erected the ceremonial buildings and the king's official quarters. Behind a third wall were the king's private quarters and the harem. Nowadays, as the king lives elsewhere and there is no harem, this innermost section is shuttered and locked.

Bangkok, once an unaspiring fishing village, became the capital of Thailand in 1782. The former capital, Ayuthia, about forty miles to the north, was conquered in 1767 by invading Burmese— so thoroughly conquered that no one was left alive to tell whether the king and his family were murdered on the spot or taken away as slaves. The treasury disappeared, the records were burned, and the charred ruins were left to the jungle. For the next fifteen years

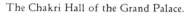

The Chakri Hall of the Grand Palace.

Europ

the Thai were ruled by a general, who managed to repel the Burmese and rally the country. It is said that he then became insane; in any event his son-in-law had him murdered and founded the dynasty that still rules Thailand, the Chakri, with himself as first king. This king, who took the name of Yot Fa, established Bangkok as his capital. As *"bang"* means village and *"kok"* means a species of wild plum, Bangkok did not seem like a very prepossessing name for a great capital, and Yot Fa thought that Krung Thep Maha Nakon Amara Ratana Kosin (Angelic City of the Precious Jewel of Indra) would sound better. Official Thai documents and maps frequently use this name, or at least Krung Thep, for short. Foreigners, however, persist in calling the city Bangkok, and only recently gave up calling the country Siam, which is a name given it by early Portuguese explorers and never used by the people who live there.

At the end of the eighteenth century Thailand was nearly as xenophobic as China and Japan. This had not always been so, however; a hundred years before, between 1680 and 1688, the most influential man in the country was a Greek. This extraordinary figure, whose name was Constantine Phaulkon, had arrived as a common seaman aboard an English ship, and remained to become prime minister and chief advisor to the king. He found Portuguese missionaries already in Ayuthia, as well as a few Dutch and English traders. While Phaulkon was prime minister, Louis XIV sent an embassy to the court at Ayuthia and, in return, Thai ambassadors were dispatched to Versailles. Things went very well until the French began demanding things, notably the conversion to Christianity of the entire Thai people. In Thailand missionaries have always been treated in a friendly manner—at Ayuthia they were even allowed to preach in the temples—but they have had remarkably little success in making Christians; even today, after hundreds of years of effort, less than five per cent of the population is Christian. The idea of forcible conversion seemed outrageous to them, and Constantine Phaulkon was suspected of being at the bottom of it. Phaulkon was killed; his friend the king died abruptly. A new government took over, and all foreigners were ordered to pack up and leave. And after that, until the middle of the nineteenth century, there was very little coming or going between Thailand and Europe. Practically the only relic of the French sojourn in Thailand is the Thai national anthem; it was composed by Louis XIV's bandmaster.

Bangkok became the richest city between India and China, and as the nineteenth century progressed, the Western powers were unable to leave it alone. In 1821 an English trade mission, sent by the governor-general of Bengal and headed by a diplomat named

Crawfurd, sailed up the Gulf of Thailand and into the Chao Phraya River. A Scottish doctor, George Finlayson, who accompanied Crawfurd, has left the first detailed account of a European's-eye view of the Grand Palace.

The English ship dropped anchor within a few miles of the palace. The welcome mat was not out. The visitors were ignored for several days and then called upon by an official whom they later found out was only of the fifth rank in importance. This official asked at once for a list of the presents for the king (they were fine cloth, glassware, muskets, and a small barouche). He then asked for, and got, an English horse that he had somehow found out was on board—it had been intended for the king of Annam, on whom the mission was to call after leaving Thailand. After further, unflattering delay, Crawfurd and a companion were taken to see a prince, who, informing them that His Majesty King Lot La had decided to receive them, wanted to make sure that they would behave properly in the royal presence. It was agreed that the Englishmen should take off their shoes at the door of the audience hall, take off their hats, bow in the English manner, sit down with "the legs bent backward and under" (to show the soles of one's feet is considered, in Thailand, very offensive), and make "three salutations with the hands united before the face, touching the forehead each time." The latter gesture is the conventional Thai greeting that serves in place of shaking hands. The higher the hands are raised before the face, the greater the obeisance, the highest position being reserved for Buddha.

On the day of the audience the king sent boats for Crawfurd, Finlayson, two other English members of the mission, and some Sepoy servants whom they had brought from Bengal. The party landed at a gate of the palace that faced the river and continued the journey in hammocks, slung between poles, from which they nearly fell out. Followed by a highly amused rabble, they proceeded to an inner gate, where, after considerable delay, they were enjoined to leave their swords and Sepoy attendants. Then they walked off toward an inner gate, this time between lines of puny boys dressed in sloppy uniforms and carrying rusty muskets "some on one side and some on the other." In front of the next gate the Englishmen, to their great annoyance, were relieved of their shoes. They now walked fifty yards in their bare feet, this time between a line of musicians playing what seemed to them "rude but not inharmonious" music, and guards who carried battle-axes and very large black shields. Thus they entered the audience hall, of which Finlayson says, "A more curious, more extraordinary, or more impressive sight has perhaps rarely been witnessed." Beneath a lofty ceiling, painted red and sprinkled all over with gold stars, were hundreds of prostrate figures lying with mouths almost touching the ground and not moving a muscle. These were the highest dignitaries of the land. At the far end of the hall was a golden curtain; as the visitors entered, this was drawn, revealing, "immovable as a statue," the king, seated upon a lofty golden throne beneath a nine-tiered golden umbrella. The guests, ordered to advance in a stooping position, seated themselves on the floor about half the hall away from the throne. The light was dim, but as their eyes grew accustomed to it, they perceived that King Lot La was a fat man of about sixty-five, wearing a close-fitting jacket of gold tissue. No crown or jewels adorned him, and Finlayson knew enough of Oriental etiquette to realize that he had left these things off purposely, in order to indicate that the mission was held in low esteem.

While large, elegant fans were waved around the base of the throne, a voice from behind the curtain read out a list of the governor-general's presents, some of which were on display. Then the king whispered something to the prostrate minister nearest him, who whispered it to the next behind him, and so down the hall, as in a children's game, until it reached the mission's interpreter. "Did you have a good trip?" "Yes, thank you." The answer went back by the same route and was succeeded by another question of equal significance. Betel was offered in silver and gold dishes, and then, after about twenty minutes, the king stood up and the curtain dropped before him, to the accompaniment of loud shouts and salutations from all present. Everyone sat up, and the audience was over. The matter of trade with Bengal had been ignored.

Outside, it had been raining, and although the way was now much dirtier than before, the visitors' shoes were withheld. "A paltry Chinese umbrella, which might be purchased in the bazaar for a rupee, was given to each of us. Not knowing with what view it was presented, I was about to reject it, when I was told that it was meant as a present from the King." Shoeless, and walking "up to the ankle in mud and water," the four were treated to a two-hour tour of the palace. First, to the stables of the white elephants—five of them, eating fresh-cut grass, sliced sugar cane, and bunches of plantains from a white cloth. They were not really white, but pinkish, with fine, scanty, yellowish hair. One of them was nearly white, with black pea-sized spots. It was explained that white elephants were reincarnations of princes or heroes and were an important source of luck for Thai rulers. The discoverer of a white elephant was granted "land equal in extent to the space of country at which the elephant's cry may be heard," and he and his family were exempted from servitude and taxation to the third generation. Next, the barefoot tourists were conducted to the temple compound, which must have looked then very much as it does now. Perhaps sore feet and general frustration had something to do with it, but they found themselves out of sympathy with Thai art. "Operose, unmeaning, and grotesque," snaps Finlayson. The temple tour concluded, the visitors were given back their shoes and offered sweetmeats. "But it was impossible to overlook the mean condition of those left to entertain us," complains Finlayson, "the disreputable appearance of the building, or the jeering and disrespectful conduct of the herd of spectators that crowded round us. It seemed as if the court had said, 'See them feed!'"

The truth gradually dawned on Crawfurd and his fellows: King Lot La was greatly offended because the mission came to him from a mere governor-general instead of from the king of England, and he was trying, in return, to be as offensive as possible. An ambassador from the King of Annam, who came to Bangkok at the same time as the Crawfurd mission, rode in the royal barge, was wined and dined, went to the audience hall in a palanquin instead of in an old hammock, and kept his shoes on. But in any event, King Lot La was not interested in foreign trade. It was enough for him that once a year a fleet of ten or twelve Thai junks, manned by Malays and Indians, went to China with sugar, pepper, sappanwood, and ironwood, and brought back chinaware and silks for the use of the court. The Thai, generally speaking, did not care for sailing, and they were a contented people, satisfied with what they found at hand. "A man who has his own rice in sufficiency, why should he want more?" says a Thai proverb. The Crawfurd mission departed in rage and frustration.

King Lot La's son, Mongkut, the first-born son of the First Queen, had been brought up in the expectation of succeeding to the throne. He was twenty years old when his father died, and happened, at that moment, to be away in a monastery, performing the temporary duties that are required of all young Buddhists. A state council was called and it was decided that Mongkut's elder half brother, child of a non-royal concubine, would make a better king by virtue of his superior age and experience. Mongkut thereupon waived his claim and spent the next twenty-seven years as a monk, while his brother, Nang Klao, ruled Thailand very much in the conservative fashion of his father. When Nang Klao died, in 1851, he named his eldest son as successor, but his ministers ignored this and named instead the forty-six year old abbot, Mongkut. It is a pleasant reflection on the peaceable nature of the Thai that both these disputable successions were accomplished without bloodshed. In contrast, in Burma as recently as 1888 an incoming king found it necessary to destroy seventy-seven close relatives.

King Mongkut, who is known in the West today chiefly as the semibarbaric, semicomic figure of "The King and I," was in fact

The king used to show himself to the people in this pavilion, built on the lower wall which separates the two main buildings of the palace.

a brilliant man and one of the most remarkable rulers the world has ever seen. During his brother's reign Thailand had stood still, as innocent as a bamboo in the jungle, while the world outside, full of startling changes, was moving ominously closer. Thailand now had two alarmingly aggressive neighbors—"the whale and the crocodile," as Mongkut once called them: England had gobbled up Burma and was busy establishing protectorates over the various sultans of the Malay States; France was encroaching on Cambodia and Annam. Mongkut, instead of putting his head in the sand as the Chinese had done, was quite aware that he had to meet the challenge of this new and threatening world. He learned English from the American missionaries in Bangkok; concluded treaties with England, the United States, and other Western powers; sent and received ambassadors; took an interest in the Paris Exhibition of 1867; and boldly hired many Western advisors, in spite of the risk of fifth-column intrigue. An Irishman had the post of drill-master; Dr. Dan Bradley, an American missionary, was court physician; Mrs. Anna Leonowens, as we all know, was royal governess; and there were a number of others. In order to insure an orderly succession, Mongkut revived an ancient Thai custom and appointed a Second King, a sort of vice-president. He gave this rank to his only full brother, a man even more outward-turning and progressive than himself, whose eldest son was named George Washington (Prince George Washington became Second King during the succeeding reign). "Our weapons will be our mouths and our hearts," said Mongkut, aware of the hopelessness of Thailand's competing in a nineteenth-century war, ". . . full of sense and wisdom for the better protection of ourselves."

Sir John Bowring, Ambassador of Queen Victoria, has left an account of his visit to the Grand Palace in 1855. The quality of the welcome he received had changed for the better, but the palace itself seems to have changed little since the days of the Crawfurd mission. There were still troops of ill-groomed soldiers, and the nobles were still supine or crawling "with their heads in the dust" in the presence of the king. Mongkut, who liked to work at night, received Bowring by moonlight. He wore a headdress of diamonds, a gold girdle, and a jeweled dagger, and inquired about the discovery of the planet Neptune, of which he had read in an English newspaper. Bowring was impressed with the king, but feared that in Thailand he was up against a system of "do-little or as little as possible." Shown around the compound of the Temple of the Emerald Buddha, he noted "a barbaric style of gorgeousness; hideous figures of every sort are stuck round." At the elephant stables he observed that the animals wore rings on their tusks and diadems on their heads, were addressed as "Chao Phya," a high title similar to "duke," went to their daily baths in the river under seven-tiered red umbrellas, and were entertained with music during their meals. Despite this delightful treatment, they were often in bad temper— perhaps because of too many sugar cakes—and had been known to stomp on their keepers. King Mongkut presented Bowring with a tuft of white-elephant hair mounted in a jeweled holder, like a Victorian nosegay.

Like his father, grandfather, and brother before him, King Mongkut maintained a large harem, locked away in the innermost regions of the palace. The harem was a self-sufficient town, populated by some three thousand women and small children and by one man, His Majesty. Policewomen, wearing blue *panungs* (loose-fitting drawers) and white jackets with a cream-colored scarf across the breast, patrolled day and night and were drilled to curtsy in unison. A policewoman accompanied any man whom it was necessary to admit, such as a repairman or a doctor. Dr. Bradley, the American court physician, was usually called, if at all, after Thai doctors had tried and failed. He found it discouraging to attend a patient whose problems had been complicated by doses of python bile or powdered vulture bone. Thai medicine was based on the premise that the body is composed of wind, water, fire, and earth, and that illness results when the balance of these four elements is disturbed. Apoplexy, for instance, was believed to be caused by wind blowing on the heart and rupturing it. Doctors did not practice surgery or autopsy, and, in fact, did not touch the patient at all, even to take the pulse. They were paid only if the patient recovered, and customarily abandoned the case if there seemed no hope of recovery, to avoid the wrath of angry relatives. "The doctor has fled the patient" means, in Thailand, that the patient is expected to die. Only royalty might die inside the palace; in case of an accidental infringement of this rule, a three-day exorcism was necessary.

Within three months of ascending the throne, Mongkut, who had been a celibate for twenty-six years, had taken thirty wives. In all, he had close to a hundred wives and concubines and eighty-two children, including twelve sired before he became a monk. Most of the wives were the daughters of noblemen, presented by their fathers, and many were closely related to Mongkut. There was no taboo, at least in royal circles, against incest. One of Mongkut's favorite queens had three daughters and all of them married Mongkut's son and successor, Chulalongkorn, their half brother.

Despite King Mongkut's earnest efforts at modernization, Chulalongkorn, in 1868, became king of a country that had no modern army, no navy at all, no general education, no legal code, no sanitation systems, no postal or telegraph service, no railways, and very few roads. Although there were some twenty-two thousand people on the palace payroll, no serious records were kept of government finances. Mongkut had introduced paper money and coinage to replace the traditional bullet-shaped silver pieces and cowrie shells, but it took a long time to coax people to use them. Mongkut had abolished *corvée* labor, but enslavement for debt continued until 1905. For the most part, royal life was still lived in a mesh of ceremonial restrictions. In 1873 one of the three sister-queens, Sunanta, was drowned when the royal barge in which she was a passenger accidentally overturned. A law forbidding anyone to touch a royal person prevented her from being rescued, although the banks were lined with hundreds of people who could swim (because of the wateriness of their country, ordinary Thai learn to swim as soon as they learn to walk). In case a royal person should be in danger of drowning, the regulations said, he should be flung a string of coconuts as a life preserver; but on that fatal day no one had a string of coconuts at hand.

The royal family was (and still is) addressed in a special, ceremonious manner, with words bequeathed by the medieval Khmers,

The king's audience hall, with the ancient boat-shaped throne.

Hundreds of frescoes depict the story of the Rama-
kien, the Thai version of the Indian epic, Ramayana.

the builders of Angkor. The ordinary Thai word for "yes" literally
translated, is "I ask to receive." The word used in saying "yes" to
royalty translates to "I in the dust beneath the soles of your august
feet ask to receive." There is no way whatsoever of saying "no" to
Thai royalty.

King Chulalongkorn had seventy-eight children by thirty-six
wives. The profusion of princes and princesses in pre-twentieth-
century Thailand had made it necessary to institute what might be
called a Law of Diminishing Titles: the grandchildren of a king
had the title of Mom Chao; great-grandchildren are known as
Mom Rachawongse; and great-great-grandchildren as Mom Luang;
generations after that are simply "Nai" or "Mr." Toward the end
of Chulalongkorn's reign a royal family party might include five
hundred near relatives. But as the three kings who followed had
no heirs, and as the present king is a monogamist, the need for the
Law of Diminishing Titles will soon have vanished.

The mother of the heir to the throne was exalted above the
other royal wives and was known as First Queen. The mother of
Chulalongkorn's heir was Saowapa, a sister of the drowned Sunanta. Saowapa and Chulalongkorn lived on the second floor of the
royal palace. The ground floor was occupied by servants, and the
third floor, which was very hot most of the year, was largely occupied by rats, mice, spiders, and *chinchooks* (small lizards that
swarm over every household in Thailand). Privacy is not much
prized in Thailand, and royalty in particular appears to have dis-

79

liked being left alone. The queen had her own bedroom, but it was always full of attendants. The children occupied a very large room that was divided off by screens into play areas and sleeping areas. Although there was some elaborate Western furniture in this palace, for the most part it merely gathered dust, Saowapa preferring to sit, eat, and sleep in the traditional Thai manner, on the floor. The king's bedroom was lavishly adorned with gold leaf. His enormous bed had curtains around it and a nine-tiered golden umbrella suspended above. On either side, at a lower level, were beds for attendants.

Chulalongkorn took care of affairs of state at night, and slept until noon or later. The windows were kept closed while he slept; outside, the gardeners went about with blowguns, shooting peas at the birds to keep them quiet. The opening of the king's window was a signal to servants waiting below to bring breakfast. Three hours later His Majesty sat down to lunch in an enormous dining room. Thirty or forty people always joined him—wives, children, and officials. His food was served in a bag tied with string and sealed with white clay, the seal being broken in the king's presence. During the meal, which went on for hours, the king found time to chat with at least some of his children. He insisted that they know the history of their dynasty, its customs and traditions; the names of the royal palaces and gateways, the royal barges, and—possibly the most difficult feat—the names of their uncles and aunts. These were arranged in rhymes to make them easier to remember.

Royal children were seldom punished. Queen Saowapa did the punishing herself, when she felt it to be necessary, either by applying a bamboo cane or by bending the children's fingers back toward the wrist. The latter punishment served the additional purpose of lengthening the wrist and finger muscles; supple joints are much admired in Thailand, and many of the movements of Thai classical dancing depend on stretched muscles. Another, rather curious, punishment was administered by the king to the wives who had had the misfortune to displease him: every day they assembled in a certain room of the second floor, the Yellow Room. There, subdued and dejected, they waited sometimes for hours, until at last Chulalongkorn would come into the room, walk slowly and silently among them, and then go out again, having absolutely ignored them all.

Often, on fine afternoons, the king went for a drive in an English victoria, while Saowapa, some minor wives, and a few dozen children followed in more carriages. The drives must have grown monotonous, for there were no roads beyond the city limits and very few in Bangkok itself. Bangkok, in those days, was a tropical Venice, and the usual way to get from place to place was either by footpath or by *klong* (canal). The fact that the king went out so often was amazing to his people. Before Mongkut, the rulers of Thailand had left the Grand Palace but once a year, at which time they visited all the temples in the city. The people had not been allowed to look at their king, but were required to shut themselves into their houses or, if caught outside, to throw themselves face downward and not peek. Mongkut had allowed himself to be looked at, and Chulalongkorn went still further and directed that the people shout hurrah. (This seemed appalling impudence to the conservative Thai, and the hurrahs were always very quiet ones.)

Sometimes, for variety, Chulalongkorn took a litle voyage on his royal steam yacht, a twenty-five-hundred-ton affair, built in England. Designed to accommodate a hundred and fifty people, it usually sailed with between four and five hundred aboard. The crew and male servants stayed forward; the harem, hidden by screens, was aft. Sometimes the ladies were allowed to disembark on a lonely island in the Gulf of Siam, where, after the yacht had re-tired discreetly over the horizon, they went sea-bathing.

Travel outside Bangkok, until the railway was completed in 1910, was by boat or elephant. A trip to Chiang Mai, Thailand's second city, took up to two months; the train cut this time to fifteen hours. When Chulalongkorn went to Chiang Mai or to an-other provincial city, he traveled in a cortege of some six hundred boats and three thousand people. He seems to have been a restless king, always journeying from one corner of his country to another. Certainly in the hot season, when cholera was usually epidemic, it was prudent to leave Bangkok. Until 1914 the city had no sanita-tion system. Water for the Grand Palace was brought in jars from a clear, swift stream fifty miles away, but the common people drank water from the river—the same river that was used as a vast mu-nicipal bathroom and dump and that, during an epidemic, often contained the bodies of cholera victims. An epidemic in 1849 caused fifteen to twenty thousand deaths in one month.

It is said that the Thai play at work and work at play. At the Grand Palace the harem women spent hours arranging bowls of fruit—peeling every grape, peeling and segmenting every orange, and then putting the grapes back into bunches and the orange seg-ments, with pips and membranes removed, back into the peel. They also knew how to sew hundreds of flower petals together to make bouquets of new, fantastic flowers or to make umbrellas or leis for Buddha images. Unlike most women in the world, they wore no headdress of any kind and their hair was clipped as short as the men's. Their teeth were black with betel (long hair and white teeth identified a whore). The time they saved by not adorning their heads went into weaving gorgeous silks for their *panungs*. Both men and women wore this comfortable, loose-fitting garment and usually went naked from the waist up—that is, until Mongkut ordered everybody into jackets. At court everyone dressed in a different color each day of the week—blue on Monday, green on Tuesday, and so on. It was the custom to sleep in one's clothes and put on fresh ones in the morning.

At the palace there was a theatrical performance nearly every night—a romantic play in poetry or a classical Thai dance for which the dancers were prepared from childhood with a training even more strenuous than that of a ballet dancer. These performances usually went on for hours, ending only when the last spectator finally left. Kite-fighting, fish-fighting, and cockroach-fighting were all serious-minded sports that took a lot of time. And there were other demanding pastimes: for example, one prince, a brother-in-law of Chulalongkorn, was particularly fond of the *victoria regia*, a water lily that opens at dusk. He did not, however, wish to smell it until midnight. Accordingly, his gardeners tied each flower with string, to hold it shut, and then, at midnight, removed the string, flooding the dark gardens with a rich, jasminelike perfume. With so much serious planning going into niceties like this, tiresome matters such as trade and finance had to wait.

The national devotion to detail, etiquette, and ceremony followed the king into death. The body of a dead king was placed, in the fetal position, inside a silver urn and this, in turn, inside a very elaborate golden one. The lid of the inner urn was sealed and the body fluids drawn off every day for two months through a stopcock in the bottom of the urn, until the body was dry. During this time the double urn was displayed in the Funeral Hall of the Grand Palace. At the end of several months a mile-long funeral procession accompanied the body to an imposing funeral pyre in the main market place, just outside the Grand Palace. After the burning of the body, remaining bits of bone were given to the late king's children, who kept them in lockets, while the ashes were put into a casket and placed in an antechamber of the Audience Hall. (When Prince William of Sweden visited Bangok in 1911, King Vajiravudh, showing him through the palace, said, "Would you like to see a bit of my father?" and opened a small golden urn. "Take hold, it won't hurt you," he said, smiling, and handed Prince William a bit of King Chulalongkorn.)

After King Chulalongkorn died, the Grand Palace ceased to be the "sun of the solar system of Siam." The next two kings, Vajiravudh and Prajadhipok, were without heirs and spent a great deal of their time building other palaces. The "inside" was inhabited now only by unmarriageable princesses—that is, princesses so royal that no one could be found who was royal enough to

Chinese junks often arrived ballasted with stone statues such as this one.

marry them. King Prajadhipok was at the seaside in 1932 when his ministers notified him that there had been a revolution and that he was no longer an absolute but a constitutional monarch. A peaceable and reasonable man in the Thai tradition, he seems to have taken this news quietly, and in 1935 abdicated in favor of a nephew, Prince Ananta-Mahidol, who was then a boy of ten at school in Switzerland. This young king died of a bullet wound in 1946—whether a case of murder, suicide, or accident has never been established. He was succeeded by his brother Bhumiphol.

King Bhumiphol, with his beautiful wife and three children, lives much as other modern monarchs live, in a palace filled with French furniture and modern conveniences. As is well known, he plays the clarinet and is an expert jazz musician, and evenings at his present palace are apt to end in impromptu jam sessions. Only on ceremonial days does he go to the Grand Palace, where he pays homage to the Emerald Buddha. And then, although they are not required to do so, his people often lie down in the dust before him, and strew his path with garlands of sewn flower petals.

83

"The Very Pearl of the Realm"
Nonsuch Palace

WHENEVER HENRY VIII ACQUIRED SOMETHING NEW IN THE WAY of a luxury, he was apt to wonder whether Francis I of France had one like it—or, Gadzooks, more of the same or better. He had met Francis only once, at the Field of the Cloth of Gold, but he had heard a great deal about all the fine things Francis had and especially about his châteaux, Chambord and Fontainebleau, which were the talk of Europe. In 1538, Henry determined to build himself a pleasure-palace that would outdo any palace in the world; and the name of this palace, therefore, would be Nonsuch.

Henry had already renovated and improved a number of his palaces and they were all brimming with expensive tapestries, gold plate, and jewels, as well as clothes made of silks and cloth of gold. But Nonsuch was the first palace that he had built from the ground up, and he intended that it should look as sumptuous on the outside as anything he might put into it. For the site, he chose the pleasant hunting country of Surrey—just twelve miles from the center of London and nearer than that to his principal residence, Hampton Court. On the spot that seemed to him ideal for his palace there happened to be a village. No matter: remove it. Several houses, a church, and a medieval churchyard were knocked down and Henry's palace begun, the drains disturbing the graves of long-dead medieval yeomen.

The plan of the palace was arrived at by a number of builders —not architects, as we know them—working under the thumb of the King. These builders were Englishmen, but among the decorators and embellishers of the palace were several Italians, some of whom had lately been in the employ of King Francis. An Italian named Toto di Nunziata, who had been in England for years and was a notable designer of stage sets and masks, probably took a hand at Nonsuch, too.

An engraving of Henry the Eighth from Raymond's *History of England.*

The appearance of palaces in sixteenth-century England was in a state of transition; the time was past when it was prudent to fortify one's residence, and yet an important house without battlements looked queer to the sixteenth-century eye. The solution was to apply battlements as ornament, and, accordingly, Nonsuch was supplied with fantastic, polygonal, five-story towers, made of gilded wood. As fortifications, of course, they would have been totally useless: they had delicate mullioned windows all around their upper stories, and their roofs were merry with carved heraldic beasts and banner-shaped vanes of painted metal. When the wind blew, the vanes must have made a pleasant, harplike sound, reminding the more erudite courtiers of Chaucer's lines:

> Alofte the toweres and golden fanes goode
> Did with the wynde make full swete armony.

The usual medieval castle had an outer and inner court, and Nonsuch followed this plan, the layout being in the shape of a squared-off "B." The lower part of the "B" was the outer court, with the entrance gate at the bottom. Here were such facilities as the buttery, the wine cellar, and the laundries. In the upper rooms were accommodations for those who held small official positions—the Cupbearer, the Almoner, the Carver, the Sewer, the Groom Porter, and so on. There were a great many of these people, and the Outer Court must have been congested and very lively. (A sixteenth-century visitor from Spain remarked that English palaces were bigger than Spanish ones, but more crowded.) Adding to the cheerful din was a multiple echo that the builders had contrived in the arches of the entrance gate. Due to certain artfully placed cavities and holes, trumpets and shouts echoed not only once but four or five times.

Of the Inner Court it may be said that there has been None Such before or since. Its walls were wooden, closely covered with scales of gilded slate. The effect of this was armorlike, and on a sunny day it all glittered and shone like some glorious dragon. Eight steps led from Outer into Inner Court, by way of a five-story gatehouse that was topped by a tremendous clock. The King and his chief courtiers looked from their windows into this court, where, besides the scales and the clock, they also saw a multitude of stucco bas-reliefs, depicting Roman and Greek myths. Around the Inner Court (that is, around one half of the "B") were the privy gardens, while before the main entrance of the palace was a bowling green. On all sides of the palace was a well-stocked deer park.

The construction of Nonsuch proceeded at full speed, often continuing through the night. Nevertheless, it was years in the building, and when Henry died, in 1547, it was still not quite finished. It was a frivolous place, and the next two rulers of England were anything but frivolous: young King Edward was too frail and worried, and Queen Mary too preoccupied with her stern purposes. Mary never went to Nonsuch, but, recognizing that it was known all over Europe as something very special indeed, she used it as a show place for visiting dignitaries and often sent important or favored persons a little present of venison from the palace's deer park. Still, after several years, she apparently felt that she did not need a piece of property like this, and sold it, in return for four other manors, plus a small cash payment—to Henry Fitzalan, Twelfth Earl of Arundel.

When Henry VIII died, the palace was placed in the care of one Sir Thomas Cawarden. Sir Thomas also bore the titles of "Master of the Revels" (*Magistrum iocorum revelorum et mascorum nostrorum*) and "Keeper of the Tents, Hales and Toyles." All this meant that he kept track of a large collection of costumes and stage sets, as well as of the tents that had to be put up whenever the court was in residence at Nonsuch—there being not nearly enough room in the palace itself for the retinue that followed the Crown. He also oversaw the deer park and kept the household inventories. Many of his bills, accounts, and business letters still exist—the English are remarkable for preserving the minutiae of history. These documents reveal that Cawarden was a Protestant and that five times, during Mary's eight-year reign, he was indicted for this crime. Unfortunately, they do not tell us how he always managed to avoid punishment. They also reveal that when Lord Arundel attempted to take possession of his new property, Cawarden proved reluctant to leave, and that "during the nut-and apple-gathering season of 1557" force of arms had to be used to push him off the premises.

Lord Arundel was a widower and a handsome, cultivated, ambitious man. After Queen Mary died, he became one of the many whose name was mentioned as a possible husband for Queen Elizabeth. In the first summer of her reign, 1559, the young Queen made a royal progress to Nonsuch, where Arundel provided her with six days of nonstop entertainment and revelry. Elizabeth thanked him graciously, accepting also as a token of his esteem a "cupboard of gilt platt," but Arundel never got any nearer to the throne. Six months later, he sent in a bill for his expenses.

Elizabeth was very fond of Nonsuch. (A contemporary noted, "Her Majesty is returned again to Nonsuch, which of all places she likes best.") On one occasion she arrived without warning, while Lord Arundel was away in Italy. She wrote to him that she had "visited your house at Nonsuche. Where we had dyvers wayes very

good contentation. And did so well ayre every parte of your house, as at your coming we thinke you shall fynde it seasonable for you.'' Years later, in 1591, she bought it from Arundel's heir, and, until her death in 1603, spent several weeks of each year there.

The gardens, inspired by Italian gardens of the period, were among the pleasantest in England. There were a hundred and forty fruit trees, a maze, and an outdoor bath, flowing with health-giving waters from a spring. There were many statues and fountains, Greek and Roman in inspiration, and an obelisk that, when passersby happened to trip a secret spring, suddenly ejected streams of water and gave them an unexpected drenching. There were so many deer that the Queen could shoot them from a pavilion in the park. And for parties on long, warm summer evenings, she could repair

This engraving, made in 1568, shows the south face of the Palace, with its
five-story corner turrets. In the foreground Queen Elizabeth sits in a plumed
coach, while on the other side of the palace a hunting party sets out.

to the banqueting house, which stood atop a little rise in the park
and overlooked the palace and its grounds.

Elizabeth was at Nonsuch in September 1599, when Robert
Dudley, Earl of Essex, returned from the wars in Ireland, where
he had disobeyed orders. He galloped down from London to see
the Queen before news of his behavior could reach her through his
enemies. It is one of the dramatic encounters of English history
and has often been described. Essex, counting on his charm and the
Queen's affection for him to extricate him from a bad situation,
burst into Her Majesty's private apartments, having ridden all

night, and found her not yet dressed—an old, vain woman caught without her wig and make-up. It could not have done his case any good. The Queen received him with a rather ominous calm; listened briefly, raised him from his knees, and told him to come back later when he had changed out of his muddy clothes. Later was too late, as Essex knew it would be. By that time, the full story of his folly in Ireland had been told to the Queen, and this folly started him along the road to the scaffold.

We can picture exactly what Nonsuch was like on that September day in 1599, because just five days previously, a traveler from the Low Countries, one Thomas Platter, had visited it and recorded many colorful details. The palace, he wrote, was set in broad green meadows, and all around it were tents, round or long, housing much of the court. "We ordered our coachman to draw up on the meadow, and alighted, and by way of a long grassy avenue enclosed by wooden palings made toward the royal palace. . . ." Platter and his party were ushered through the Outer and Inner Courts and into the Royal Presence Chamber. This was hung with fine tapestries, and the floor strewn with straw or hay, except for Turkish carpets where Her Majesty was to step. Surrounded by kneeling ladies in waiting, guards, and courtiers, the Queen, "very straight and erect," sat on a low seat covered with red damask and gold, with a canopy above her head. She wore white satin with gold embroidery, and on her head "a whole bird of paradise as a panache," studded with jewels. She also wore huge round pearls, and several glittering rings on gloved hands. It was Sunday and a preacher was standing before her, delivering a sermon. " . . . She listened, not for long, however, for since it was very warm and late and many people were assembled, she called one of the knights to come to her and commanded him while he knelt before her to sign to the preacher to draw to a close, as the time was going on."

Then she withdrew, and the visitors were invited to watch lunch being served. Guardsmen wearing red tabards with the Queen's arms embroidered in gold on the back, carried in tables and trestles. After that, forty more guardsmen entered, each bearing a dish. A lady in waiting cut a portion from each offering ("large joints of beef, all kinds of game, pastries and tarts") and gave it to the guard who had carried the dish. Then the dishes were sent in to the Queen, accompanied by flagons of wine and beer, while musicians played to the empty table. After this, Platter and his friends were taken back to the tents and given a lunch of their own, for which they must have been extremely hungry.

After Elizabeth died, Nonsuch began a long, slow decay. James I called it "a lavish place of nonsense," and gave it to his unbeloved wife, Anne of Denmark, who seldom went there. Charles

I did not care for it, either. Times and tastes had changed, and Nonsuch, with its exuberant stucco decoration and its gorgeous, glittering scales, was out of style. "The very pearl of the realm," a sixteenth-century writer had called it; there had even been a "school of Nonsuch" in architecture, in furniture, and in elaborate interior carvings, such as chimney pieces. But now, in the seventeenth century, the old place was generally dismissed as a monstrosity.

This view was printed in 1610 in a corner of Speed's map of Surrey. Part of the wall on the left could be let down to form a stage.

Oddly enough, the sobersided Cromwellians liked it. After the execution of Charles I and the establishment of the Commonwealth, appraisers were sent down to see if the palace had any practical use. The resulting "Parliamentary Commissioners Report" of 1650, shows enthusiasm beyond the call of duty. The "frontespeece" of the palace, the commissioner reported, was "railed in with strong and handsome rayles and ballasters of freestone." From the park gate to the "frontespeece" (the gate of the Outer Court) ran "two faire ranks of trees." The commissioners particularly admired the plumbing—a lead cistern in the west turret from which water was piped throughout the royal apartments. In the privy gardens,

Country Li

The three painted canvas panels now in Losely Park,
Guildford, Surrey, are believed to have come from Nonsuch.

they found an unfamiliar bush called "leylack," and perhaps did
not quite approve of it, noting that it bore "no fruit but only a
very pleasant flower." The materials of the palace were evaluated at
£7020, but the commissioners emphasized that the palace was
"fitt for present use" and should not "bee demolished or taken
downe." Thomas Pride of "Pride's Purge" lived comfortably at
a house in Nonsuch Park from 1652 until his death in 1658.
Whether it was an easeful death has not been recorded; had he lived
two years longer, he would have shared the fate of many of his fel-
low-regicides and been hanged, drawn, and quartered.

When Charles II came to the throne, he, too, stayed away
from Nonsuch. Perhaps it struck him as a nice, old-fashioned place
of retirement for an old lady, because he turned it back to his
mother, the Dowager Queen Henrietta Maria, who had owned it
during Charles I's lifetime. She, however, preferred her native
France. In 1665, during the Great Plague in London, the Office of
the Exchequer moved hastily to Nonsuch, bag and baggage; and
the Surveyor General of the Victualling Office, who, as it happened,
was Samuel Pepys, had several occasions to go there. "A fine place

92

it hath heretofore been," he wrote in his diary. On one occasion he "walked into the ruined garden," where, not unpredictably, he made the acquaintance of a young girl, " . . . a plain little girle, to sing very finely by the eare only, but a fine way of singing, and if I come ever to lacke a girle again I shall think of getting her."

The other great English diarist of the seventeenth century, John Evelyn, visited Nonsuch in January 1666 and wrote "I supped in None-such House . . . and tooke an exact view of the plaster statues and bass-relievos inserted twixt the timbers and puncheons of the outside walls of the Court . . . admire I did much how it lasted so well and intire as since the time of Henry VIII, exposed as they are to the aire; and pitty it is they are not taken out and preserved in some dry place; a gallerie would become them. These are some mezzo-relievos as big as the life, and the storie is of the Heathen Gods. . . . The palace consists of 2 courts, the first is of stone, castle-like . . . the other of timber, a Gothic fabric, but these walls incomparably beautified." He also noted that "scales of slate . . . preserved it from rotting like a coate of armour."

When the Exchequer moved to Nonsuch, all sorts of overdue repairs were pushed forward—new slates for the roof, new windowpanes, and so on. As in many a superannuated mansion of our day, humble office clerks now found themselves at work in surroundings of decayed splendor. In the vast rooms, thin partitions were thrown up to make offices; and instead of the notes of lute and lyre and hunting horn, the principle sound was the scratching of quill pens. When the Plague was over, the Exchequer went back to Westminster, but returned again, even more precipitously than before, when the Great Fire of London broke out (September 2, 1666).

After the death of Henrietta Maria, in 1669, the King decided to give Nonsuch to one of his mistresses, Barbara Villiers, Countess of Castlemaine. Barbara had been his mistress for a number of years; his eye was roving, and the gift of Nonsuch was in the nature of a divorce settlement. At the same time, he also made her countess of Southampton and Duchess of Cleveland, as well as Baroness of Nonsuch. Her eldest son by the King (she had had three royal bastards) and his male heirs were to inherit the property and titles. Various revenues came with all this and would have taken care of the Duchess handsomely had she not been fatally fond of gambling. A country house in constant need of repair was the last thing to interest her. She moved to Paris, where the gaming tables sat late and the stakes were high, and she ignored Nonsuch, which for a number of years had been under the official care of the Earl of Berkeley. Then, on one disastrous evening in 1679, she lost £20,000 and all her jewelry. After that she was always hard-pressed for cash, and in 1682 decided to tear down Nonsuch and sell every stick of it for whatever she could get. The Earl of Berkeley, however, behaving curiously like Sir Thomas Cawarden a hundred years before, now threw countless obstacles, legal and physical in the way of the Duchess's emissaries when they came to pull down the palace and "dispark" the park. On one occasion he even fended off an armed sally by one of her royal sons, the Duke of Grafton. Then, quite suddenly—there must have been behind-the-scenes forces at work—Berkeley accepted the arrears salary that was due him and moved meekly out. In a short time there were only ruins where "the very pearl of the realm" had stood.

What became of all the rubble? The Duchess sold most of it to a builder for £1,700. Berkeley took some of the plaster reliefs, some building stone, and various odds and ends to use at his new and elegant manor, Durdans; some painted panels, still to be seen at a manor near Guildford, are believed to come from Nonsuch, and so are a few chests and chimney pieces of extravagant design; lead was melted down; stone and timber turned up for years after in the walls of the villages roundabout. An eighteenth-century writer, extolling the attractions of the health spa of Epsom, remarked that the houses had been "beautified by the owners to the utmost of their ability, to which the ruins of Nonsuch Palace have contributed not a little."

Within a century, astonishing as it seems, the palace had disappeared so completely that no one could even say where it had stood. The park was kept up, first by a private owner and then by public funds, but not so much as a stone of the palace remained above ground. Then, in 1959, the British Ministry of Works decided to excavate the site; and it took resolute delving into old records to determine the proper place to dig. An army of the Ministry's workmen, assisted by student and amateur archaeologists and supervised by professionals, laid bare the foundations of the palace, as well as the earlier foundations of the village and churchyard that Henry VIII had toppled to make room for his palace. Besides a wealth of broken sixteenth-century pottery and glass, and parts of the famous stucco bas-reliefs, there also came to light over a hundred medieval skeletons.

For three months of that summer, the foundations lay exposed to view; then, because of the difficulty and expense of preserving them, they were covered up again. The finds, including the bones, were taken away and catalogued. Now that the voices of courtiers and workmen, kings and queens and archaeologists all have died away, perhaps the skeletons will be allowed to resume the sleep that Henry interrupted.

The Marble Cottages
Newport Houses of the Vanderbilts

HENRY JAMES, LOOKING BACK ON THE NEWPORT HE KNEW IN
the 1860s, compared it to "a little bare, white, open hand, with
slightly-parted fingers." In those days Newport was both a fishing
port and a summer resort for quiet, intellectual families from Boston—the Longfellows, the Jameses, and the Howes, to name a few
—as well as for yachting enthusiasts from New York and Southern
aristocrats in search of Northern summer breezes. Although some
of these people possessed very substantial fortunes, ostentation was
anathema to them and what they liked about Newport was its
simplicity.

"It is the back of the hand, rising to the swell of the wrist,
that is exposed," James went on, "which is the way, I think, the
true lover takes and admires it. He makes out in it . . . innumerable
shy and subtle beauties . . . and he winces at the sight of certain
other obtruded ways of dealing with it." But, beginning in the
eighties, the hand began to be roughly treated by parvenu obtruders
who apparently had no sense of the delicate thing they were dealing with. "The pink palm being empty, in other words, to their
vision, they had begun, from far back, to put things into it, things
of their own, and of all sorts, and of many ugly, and of more and
more expensive, sorts; to fill it substantially, that is, with gold, the
gold that they have ended by heaping up there to an amount so
oddly out of proportion to the scale of nature and of space." James,
a gentleman before he was a journalist, did not name any of these
persons who did not care for empty hands; had he done so, his list
would certainly have been topped by the name of Vanderbilt, although he might have had trouble deciding *which* Vanderbilt—
whether Mr. and Mrs. Cornelius II, whose "cottage," The Breakers,
had four stories and seventy rooms, or Mr. and Mrs. William K.,
who, although their "Marble House" was only about the size of the

Petit Trianon, had spent nine million dollars on its furnishings and had given a coming-out ball for their daughter Consuelo that, in the view of *The New York Times* of August 31, 1895, "outdid any private social function ever given in this country."

Heydays are often brief, but the heyday of Marble House and The Breakers lasted, in comparison to those of other palaces, about as long as a sneeze. Marble House was built first, being completed in 1892; the following spring the Cornelius Vanderbilts began The Breakers, and it was finished in 1895. For one glorious Newport season both houses were open and their owners hard at work entertaining. (Said Alva, wife of William K.: "I know of no profession, art, or trade that women are working in today as taxing on mental resource as being a leader of Society.") But, by the following summer, Cornelius Vanderbilt II was ill and did very little entertaining, while Alva and William K. were divorced and Alva was engaged to be married to another millionaire, Oliver H. P. Belmont, who lived just down the street in a Louis XIII hunting lodge called Belcourt. William K. went abroad in his yacht. On becoming Mrs. Belmont, Alva closed Marble House—though she continued to have her washing and ironing done there, Belcourt being rather short on housekeeping facilities. Cornelius Vanderbilt II died in 1899, and after that the two Vanderbilt palaces were closed much more frequently than they were open.

By this time there was a considerable herd of these white elephants in Newport. To quote James once more: "They look queer and conscious and lumpish—some of them with an air of the brandished proboscis, really grotesque—while their averted owners, roused from a witless dream, wonder what in the world is to be done with them. The answer to which, I think, can only be that there is absolutely nothing to be done; nothing but to let them stand there always, vast and blank, for reminder of the prohibited degrees of witlessness."

James would be startled if he could see them now—vast still, but far from blank. All summer long they swarm with guided tours, and on an occasional evening are lighted again for a musicale or a ball to which anyone can come who wants to buy a rather expensive ticket in a worthy cause. As sober reminders of "the prohibited degrees of witlessness" they are probably not very useful, for witlessness today takes other forms and Marble House and The Breakers are too far removed from our world to be anything but curiosities.

Newport's metamorphosis was due chiefly to the fact that the prime status symbol for a nineteenth-century millionaire was a yacht, and the spanking breezes of Narragansett Bay showed a yacht off uncommonly well. Beginning in the seventies, the fishing boats and obsolete whaling vessels of Newport Harbor were joined by steam yachts so stately that they could cross the Atlantic. Aboard one of them the French writer Paul Bourget encountered old-rose damask draperies, a piano, an aviary of exotic birds, a dining table groaning under crystal, silver, and orchids, and "Negroes stationed banjo in hand." The skippers of such vessels naturally needed an appropriate place to lay their heads while on land, and thus the simple dwellings of the Rhode Island shore began to give way to mansions. The new houses were called "cottages," and indeed resembled cottages except in size, being made of shingles or rough-hewn granite. But very soon these seemed inadequate for the grand people who lived in them.

"Up to this time," wrote Ward McAllister, the social arbiter of New York and Newport, in 1890, "for one to be worth a million of dollars was to be rated as a man of fortune, but now, bygones must be bygones." Fifty or a hundred million was more like it, and "fashion demanded that you be received in the hall of the house in which you were to dine by from five to six servants, who, with the butler, were to serve the repast."

There was only a handful of families rich enough to meet Ward McAllister's requirements, and even fewer who wanted to; one of these was the Vanderbilts. Old Commodore Vanderbilt, born in a shack on Staten Island in the last years of the eighteenth century, had amassed one hundred and five million dollars, but he had not cared for Society—nor it for him. At his death in 1877, he left the bulk of his fortune to his second son, William Henry, who promptly escalated it to two hundred million. When *he* died in 1885, he was the richest man in the world (a contemporary observer noted that his fortune, converted into gold, would have weighed five hundred tons). He left the equivalent of two hundred and fifty tons apiece to his two sons, Cornelius and William Kissam. Social prestige depended on the wife: William Henry had improved his social status by marrying the daughter of a Brooklyn minister of good family. His sons went all the way and chose wives who were belles of High Society: Alice Gwynne became the bride of Cornelius, and Alva Smith, of Mobile, the bride of William. Each wife took her position with enormous gravity, but their characters were quite different and they disliked each other. Alice was a Queen Mary, sure of her rank, tolerating no breaches of etiquette or tradition. Alva burned with ambition: "I always do everything first," said she. "I blaze the trail for the rest to walk in. I was the first girl of my set to marry a Vanderbilt."

She was also the first of her set to marry her daughter to a duke, as well as the first to sue her husband for divorce, marry again, and still retain her social position. Later in life, as Mrs. O. H. P.

Brown Brothers

Bettmann Archive, Inc.

LEFT: Mr. and Mrs. Cornelius Vanderbilt on their way to a fancy-dress ball in 1883. ABOVE: Mrs. O. H. P. Belmont. RIGHT: Mr. W. K. Vanderbilt and his daughter Consuelo, the Duchess of Marlborough, at the races in Paris.

Belmont, she became an agitator for women's rights, and gave a follower the famous advice "call on God and She will help you." When, in 1926, her daughter, Consuelo, Duchess of Marlborough, asked the Sacred Rota for an annulment on the grounds that her mother had forced her into the marriage, Alva became probably the first mother publicly and in writing to admit such a thing. "I forced my daughter to marry the Duke," she testified. "I have always had absolute power over my daughter, my children having been entrusted to me entirely after my divorce. When I issued an order, nobody discussed it. I therefore did not beg, but ordered her to marry the Duke." Whom Alva had joined together, the Rota put asunder.

In 1932 Alva sold Marble House to Frederick Prince, died (aged eighty), and retired to a tomb of her own design in Woodlawn. A suffragette banner flown at her funeral bore the legend "Failure Is Impossible." In addition to the tomb, Alva had designed a number of houses—all palaces, of course, and all for herself. The architect whose work she most liked to superintend was

Richard Morris Hunt. One of his jobs for the Vanderbilts had been the family mausoleum on Staten Island, which, as requested by William H. Vanderbilt, was "roomy and solid and rich." For Alva and William K., the architect had designed a palatial New York town house at 660 Fifth Avenue, comprising elements of late French Gothic, early French Renaissance, and Loire Valley romantic classicism. It pleased its owners very much. Thus, in 1888, when William K. decided to give his wife a new summer place as a birthday present, Hunt suggested something along the lines of the Petit Trianon. They put him to work at once.

Hunt, the brother of the American romantic painter William Morris Hunt, came from a prosperous Vermont family and had spent more than a decade of his youth studying in France. A Francophile, he believed passionately that the only good architecture for America was that based on French models. Like Alva, he was a tireless worker, and, fortunately, he had no objection to subordinating his own ideas to those of his employers. "If they want you to build a house upside down, standing on its chimney, it's up to you to do it and still get the best possible result," he once said. This combination of industry, amenability, and a highly knowledgeable taste for the most extravagant flights of architecture known to man made him the ideal architect for Mrs. Alva Vanderbilt, while the fact that she enabled him to actually build French palaces, not just admire them, made her the ideal patroness for Hunt.

Marble House took three years to build, from 1889 to 1892. So many carvings, rare marbles, and other objects of art were sent over from Europe that the Vanderbilts needed their own wharf, warehouse, and ten-ton derrick. Newport townspeople became used to hearing foreign chatter in their streets: they knew it came from either a fortune-hunting count or a Vanderbilt marble cutter.

The style of the house is more Louis XIV than anything else, with Louis's sunray emblem turning up frequently and a portrait of the Sun King himself hanging over the fireplace in the dining room, looking down, perhaps covetously, on the only set of solid bronze dining chairs in the world. The drawing room drops back in time a couple of hundred years and turns Gothic, complete with linen-fold paneling and a crenelated chimney piece. It was in this exceptionally gloomy room—the windows were then paned in stained glass—that the Duke of Marlborough is said to have proposed to Miss Consuelo. The grand stair well, forty feet high, was decorated by Karl Bitter, an Austrian immigrant discovered by Hunt, who later designed the fountain at Fifth Avenue and Fifty-ninth Street in New York and the façade of the Metropolitan Museum of Art. The William K. Vanderbilts had him make a bas-relief likeness of Hunt, together with one of Hardouin-Mansart, the architect who completed Versailles, and include them both among the embellishments of Marble House's stair landing.

To the left of the landing is "Mr. Vanderbilt's sitting room" (Louis XV: red damask, tapestries, and bronzes) and to the right is "Mrs. Vanderbilt's sitting room" (rococo: marquetry and ormolu, cherubs and garlands). For her bedroom Mrs. Vanderbilt clung to the more untrammeled aspects of rococo—swags, tassels, pink-and-blue ceiling frescoes, and pastel portraits of imaginary eighteenth-century swells; while her husband, in his much smaller bedroom, chose (or had chosen for him) a more sobersided Louis XVI style, in a color scheme of dark green, purple, and bronze doré.

The Corinthian columns that support the front portico are the size of those of the Temple of Jupiter at Baalbek (and those were the largest known to antiquity); the ironwork gate is copied from that at Versailles; and the whole inadequate plot of ground is surrounded by a marble wall—one of the first walls to intrude upon Newport, which had always prized the old-fashioned American concept of unfenced lawns.

One rather curious feature of the house was that it had no doorknobs on the outside. To get in, one had either to have a key or to be admitted. The kitchen and servants' quarters were all belowstairs, and a heavy door, like the door to a safe-deposit vault, kept the servants from erupting into the house when not sent for. A flunky was always on duty at the door to count them in and out.

No sooner was Marble House put together than the large but unelaborate Newport residence of the Cornelius Vanderbilts burned down, and Hunt was engaged to replace it. Cornelius Vanderbilt II was much more interested in business than in Society and had trouble staying awake at parties, but willy-nilly he became the owner of the most expensive and stately pleasure-dome that the North American continent had yet seen—The Breakers. It was the Marble House story all over again, but intensified—more imported marble, more imported stonecutters and ironworkers and parquet fitters, more gilt, damask, and cut velvet, more tapestries, more allegorical frescoes. Hunt took his inspiration from a Genoese merchant prince's villa of the early Renaissance, and perhaps the most attractive feature of the house is a wide Italianate loggia overlooking the sea. Big enough to accommodate more merchant princes than Genoa ever saw, it must have been an exceedingly pleasant place for a quiet rest on a hot summer day.

Ships arrived from Europe with entire cargoes consigned to Mr. Vanderbilt. The Breakers' music room was designed and executed down to the last detail in France and shipped in packing cases, like a prefabricated house, along with the workmen to put it up. To make this palace supremely fireproof, no wood was used in its construction and the furnace room was placed underground some hundreds of feet away. Electric lighting not being entirely reliable in those days, the whole house had gas fixtures as well; the bathrooms offered a choice of fresh or salt hot and cold running water. Someone had thought up a coat of arms for the Vanderbilts—oak leaves and acorns—and this proved handy for filling in empty spaces. (Unkind observers have remarked that the Vanderbilts paneled and muraled the walls of their houses so lavishly because they were shy of ancestral portraits; but Alice Gwynne Vanderbilt had enough likenesses of earlier Gwynnes on hand to adorn the library. Also in the library is a mantelpiece that came out of a sixteenth-century chateau and bears an inscription in archaic French, "I laugh at riches and do very well without them, since what really matters is cleverness.")

The greatest difficulty with these brand-new palaces was to keep them from looking new. Sod could be brought over from England and quickly made to seem as if it had been there for centuries, but no amount of Vanderbilt money could get a big oak out

The front of Marble House, showing the huge Corinthian columns. Many kinds and colors of marble were used for the building's construction and decoration.

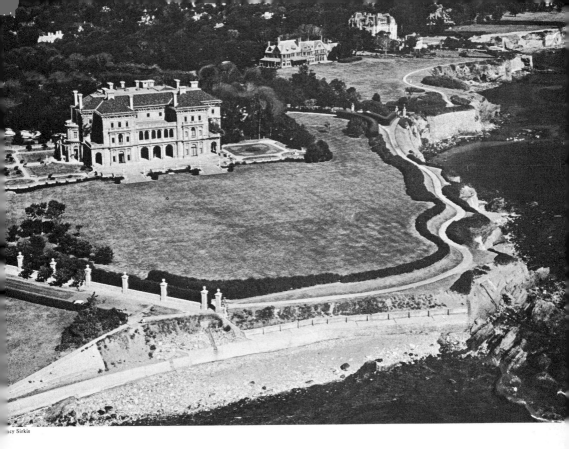

Aerial view showing The Breakers and some of its neighbors—"so oddly out of proportion," said Henry James, "to the scale of nature and space."

of a little acorn any faster than God intended. Thirty-ton trees were, therefore, hauled in and planted at a cost of nine hundred dollars a tree, but they often failed to thrive in the continual sea wind. It was a difficulty shared by all Newport's "cottagers," and when property changed hands, a departing owner often took his trees with him, for they represented a separate and considerable investment. Perhaps to draw attention away from the tree shortage, the Newport elite vied with one another over the magnificence of their flower beds and floral arrangements: newspaper accounts of parties always included long, awed paragraphs about the flowers and how much they had cost. At Consuelo's debut in the summer of 1895, for example, the hall of Marble House was banked with fifteen-foot hollyhocks aflutter with artificial butterflies and bees; and when in the following year the Cornelius Vanderbilts' daughter, Gertrude, was married to Harry Payne Whitney at The Breakers, the grand hall was a bower of eight-foot rose trees.

And what was day-to-day life like, once the mansions were built, the servants in their livery, the foliage in place, and the lights turned on? Whatever else it may have been, it was strenuous. In the mornings the ladies visited, watched or played tennis, and held parlays with their chefs, gardeners, and housekeepers; the gentlemen sailed, swam, or played polo, or repaired to the Newport Reading Room, possibly to read. Luncheons were at two, followed by bridge or more sports, active or spectator. On the servants' day off, it was possible to watch a cricket match, for there were so many English servants in Newport that they had organized a cricket club. From five to sunset there was driving on the avenues. "Fashionable women give pet names to their automobiles or electric carriages," reported Mrs. John King van Rensselaer in her book *The Social Ladder*. "Some are called Puff-puff. Another is familiarly named Angelica, while a third is called Toby." Dinner parties were at eight, followed by music or cards. But unless there was a ball, evenings ended early, and the whole glittering, elegant resort closed up as guilelessly as a morning-glory. This astounded foreign visitors, for whom the best hours of the day were the late ones. One beautiful Newport debutante told the Frenchman Paul Bourget that sometimes when her carriage was late in fetching her from a dinner party, she went to sleep in the dressing room of the house where she had been dining "rather than return to the drawing room, knowing as I did that my poor hosts were tired, too." For this dreary state of affairs Bourget blamed too much fresh air and exercise.

The press, in that era, was generally respectful in speaking of the exalted doings of the rich; reports of debuts, balls, and weddings were lovingly detailed, and on the front page, too. One musicale given by a Vanderbilt was said to have cost ten thousand dollars; twenty chefs had worked several days on the refreshments, which included a centerpiece made of seven hundred sugared almonds worked into the shape of an owl. At Consuelo Vanderbilt's debut Alva wore pale green satin and Spanish lace, with multiple ropes of Oriental pearls running over one shoulder and under the other arm. The favors alone cost five thousand dollars and included working bagpipes covered in blue velvet and large oars with silver blades. The editor of *Town Topics* (a weekly magazine that, unlike the daily press, was not at all respectful) spiced his reportage with caustic comments: Marble House, he said, had formerly been called The Marble Heart, but after the debut ball it could change its name to The Glad Hand. "I am told that some of the women at Mrs. Vanderbilt's ball . . . stole favors from each other whenever they could and particularly the more expensive ones." Gertrude Vanderbilt Whitney "made a handsome picture at her wedding although not, strictly speaking, a really handsome girl."

The public was eager to know how much life in Newport cost, and *Cosmopolitan*, in an early twentieth-century issue, tried to oblige. A yacht, it said, came to $20,000 a month, while for household staff the tab was generally about $23,800 a year: $5,000 a year for a French chef, and so on down through the secretary ($3,000), governess ($1,000), head gardener ($1,000), butler ($900), and five maids at $250 a year each. The Vanderbilts, however, paid *their* French chef $10,000, and maintained a far bigger staff than ordinary millionaires.

Yearly clothes bills for an average Newport society leader were broken down by *Cosmopolitan* as follows (and present-day readers should remember that the dollar was then worth a great deal more than it is now):

Furs	$ 5,000
Dinner gowns	5,000
Ball and opera gowns	8,000
Cloaks, wraps	2,500
Afternoon, visiting, and luncheon toilettes	3,000
Morning, shirtwaists, and informal	3,000
Automobiling furs and costumes	2,000
Negligées	800
Lingerie	1,500
Hats, veils	1,200
Riding habits	750
Shoes	800
Hosiery	500
Fans, laces, small jewels	2,500
Gloves	450
Cleaning	1,000
Handkerchiefs	600
	$38,600

For men, too, dressing was a demanding business. Here, for example, is what Mr. Henry C. Clews, Jr., wore to the international tennis tournament in Newport at about the turn of the century: a suit of purplish gray cheviot; a double-breasted waistcoat of brocaded purple satin; a long, flowing scarf of a bit brighter shade of purple; a white felt hat banded with heavy folds of purple corded silk; and, as a boutonniere, a lavender hydrangea.

As the twentieth century was born and grew to its teens, life in High Society became more and more complex. It was still important to be seen at Newport every season ("as imperative for a social aspirant's claims" declared a book called *The Ultra-Fashionable*

Peerage of America in 1904, "as it was for a potentate of the era of Charlemagne to go to St. Peter's, Rome, for coronation"). But it was also important to be seen (and recognized and invited to parties) in Paris, London, Vienna, the leading German spas, and New York. The society leader Mrs. John R. Drexel remarked that this business of having to keep *en évidence* the year round was enough to make Society women "drop down in harness."

And so the behemoth cottages along Bellevue Avenue became less and less lived in. After O. H. P. Belmont died in 1908, Alva moved back into Marble House, but she rarely entertained as she had in the nineties. She even threw it open to the common hordes for women's rights rallies. In July of 1914, when her daughter, the Duchess, was visiting her, she gave one last old-fashioned, hang-the-expense ball. In honor of a Chinese teahouse newly constructed on the grounds, the motif of the ball was Chinese, with the hostess in a three-hundred-year-old ceremonial robe said to have belonged to an empress of China, and the Duchess in embroidered silk pajamas. But that was the last of the great Marble House parties. The coming of the First World War, scarcely a month later, put a damper on all-out merrymaking. But more devastating to Marble House and The Breakers than any war was the legal bomb that had been dropped in Congress the year before: the adoption of the Sixteenth Amendment, and the inauguration of the income tax.

After the war was over, Newport's old grandeur came back for a while, but never on the scale of the nineties. Marble House was boarded up during most of the twenties. In the thirties, when it was owned by Frederick Prince of Boston, its lights winked on from time to time, only to die again with the death of Mr. Prince. The Breakers eventually came into the hands of the Cornelius II's youngest daughter, who had been a little girl when it was built. This was Countess Gladys Széchényi (she, like many American heiresses of the time, had married a foreign nobleman). When she died, in January 1965, ownership of The Breakers passed to The Preservation Society of Newport County. Until her death the Countess visited Newport each summer, just as she had been brought up to do, but, unlike Mrs. Drexel, she was not *en évidence*. Quite the opposite—she was in seclusion on the third floor of The Breakers, her presence unsuspected by the tourists thronging the lower rooms.

The architect, Hunt, had been criticized when he built The Breakers for giving it a third floor, on the grounds that this made the house out of proportion to the land around it. Little did he, or anyone, imagine how useful this third floor would be someday.

The Grand Seraglio

Topkapi Seray, Istanbul

TRAVELERS WHO ARRIVE IN ISTANBUL BY SEA HAVE A GOOD view of the Grand Seraglio: a huddle of low, unprepossessing gray buildings built on a bluff at the point where the Bosporus and the Golden Horn meet the Sea of Marmara. Nearby, and outbidding it for attention, are the six spectacular minarets of the Blue Mosque and the great dome and minarets of Aya Sophia—the ornaments of the Istanbul sky line and the great attractions for sight-seers. A tourist who asks about the low gray buildings will be told that they are the Topkapi Museum; with luck, he will also learn that until 1851 this was the Sultans' residence, a palace known to Europeans as the Grand Seraglio. But the chances are that a tourist of no more than average inquisitiveness will never learn that this palace was once more splendid than Versailles, more bloody than the Kremlin, and, though in Europe, as mysterious to Europeans as the Imperial Palace in Peking. Its extraordinary history changed millions of lives, from the Arabian peninsula halfway across Europe and the Mediterranean, and took place among brainwashed slaves behind an iron curtain that remained drawn from shortly after the conquest of Constantinople, in 1453, to the middle of the nineteenth century.

The Marmara side of Seraglio Point, a steep, four-hundred-foot ascent, was once guarded by a sea wall built of Byzantine rubble, but the wall is tumbled down now to make way for a railway, and gypsies and beggars live in the ruins. The other side of the point slopes down to the Golden Horn, which is now a raffish dock area, but in the days of the Sultans was beautiful with palaces and gardens. The unadorned stone buildings of the palace, clustered and sprawled together without aesthetic consideration, suggest a military camp; the tented armies of the Seljuk Turks must have camped like this as they swept across Anatolia from the Asiatic steppes. To modern visitors the whole palace, inside and out, seems drab and rattletrap, and it is hard to understand how the seventeenth-century French traveler Michel Baudier could have reported "the baths, halls and galleries of this place surpass in their Magnificence the force of the imagination." Few travelers from the West in those days ever got inside the palace, and fewer still got out again. Trespassers anywhere on the premises were beheaded, while trespassers in the harem were skinned alive and their skins tacked to the harem gate; but before they died they undoubtedly agreed with Baudier: the place was dumbfoundingly splendid.

"Now come with me," wrote a fifteenth-century French ambassador, "and cast your eye over the immense crowd of turbaned heads, wrapped in countless folds of the whitest silk, and bright raiment of every kind and hue, and everywhere the brilliance of gold, silver, purple, silk and satin." Lady Mary Wortley Montagu, who passed that way in 1717 when her husband was a British envoy, wrote that the royal gardeners were so gaily dressed that "at a distance they appeared like a parterre of tulips." Entertained at dinner by a wife of the Sultan, Lady Mary observed among the trinkets her hostess was wearing "200 emeralds, every one as large as a halfcrown piece," and four strings of pearls, "every one as large as the Duchess of Marlborough's." The knives were of gold set with diamonds and the tablecloth and napkins were embroidered with silk and gold.

The significant point about the Turkish court seems to be that its dazzle was not created by architecture, which had no particular appeal to a race so recently out of tents in Central Asia, but by the portable grandeur inside the buildings. The silks have worn out, the gold and jewels have been nearly all dispersed, and the Grand Seraglio, where three centuries of extraordinary drama were enacted, comes down to us as a bare, dark stage.

Except for the Sultan and his children, every soul in the Grand Seraglio—even the Grand Vizier, the General of the Armies, and the Queen Mother—was a slave, and not one of them was a Turk by birth. They were brought to the palace as children, between the ages of ten and fourteen. The girls were obtained through slave dealers and the boys, under a law of the land, were kidnapped from subject Christian states in lots of two to three thousand every three or four years. The most intelligent, most prepossessing boys were taken, and their kidnapping was by no means always opposed by their parents, for a place at the Sultan's court was the one available route to wealth and power.

The brightest of these bright children were enrolled in the Palace School inside the Grand Seraglio. Here they underwent a twelve-year brainwashing from which, if they survived, they

A portrait of Sultan Mohammed II, conqueror of Constantinople, and
first builder of the Grand Seraglio, painted by Gentile Bellini in 1479.

emerged oblivious of their earlier life, devoted to the sultanate, and fanatical followers of Islam. A seventeenth-century Venetian, Ottaviano Bon, reported of this school, "There is great severity used in all the orders of discipline, the government of them being in the hands of the masters, who are all white eunuchs for the most part, and very rough and cruel in all their actions; insomuch that when one cometh out of that Seraglio, and hath run through all the orders of it, he is, without all question, the most mortified and patient man in the world; for the blows which they suffer, and the fastings which are commanded them for every small fault, are to be admired: nay, some of them are so cruelly handled, that although their time of being in the Seraglio be almost expired, and that they should in a few years come forth to be made great men, yet not being able to endure such cruelty any longer, they procure to be turned out, contenting themselves with the title, and small pay of a Spahee or a Mutaferraka [common soldier] rather than be so often punished and made weary of their lives."

The first thing the new students learned was to keep quiet, for in the inner palace, where the school was, only the Sultan might speak above a whisper. From the Sultan's mutes the boys learned sign language. "Both the Grand Signor, and divers that are about him," said Bon, "can reason and discourse with the Mutes of any thing as well and as distinctly *alla Mutescha*, by nods and signs, as they can with words; a thing well befitting . . . the gravity of the better sort of Turks, who cannot endure much babbling."

The academic system was excellent, but for the ultimate welfare of the Turkish Empire it had one fatal flaw: it ignored the West. The boys learned Turkish, Arabic, Persian, and Tartar; athletics, riding, and warfare; and each acquired a special skill such as hawk-keeping or turban-folding. According to the Koran, "He who learns is the dearly beloved friend of Allah," and a state law required that every Turk, including the Sultan, should learn how to do something. Mohammed II, the conqueror of Constantinople, was an accredited gardener, and Abdul Hamid II did cabinetwork.

During their training the boys acted as pages. After graduation they became eligible for positions of trust: Private Secretary, Chief Huntsman, Chief Barber, Chief Accountant, Chief Bath Attendant, and so on. If they were gay and amusing fellows, they might become Boon Companions, who hunted with the Grand Seigneur, read to him, and tried to keep him amused. Eventually they might hope to receive the title of pasha and be sent out to govern a province or to spy on some other provincial governor, for the government was a network of spies and counterspies, with the chief officials in a constant welter of plotting against one another and obtaining one another's downfall. "He that is even greatest in

110

Engraving of the Seraglio from Percival Barlow's *General History of Europe*.

office is but a statue of glass," says a Turkish proverb. A popular
Turkish curse still is "Mayst thou be vizier to Sultan Selim," for
during the eight-year reign of Selim the Grim seven Grand Viziers
(prime ministers) lost their heads.

When Sultans decided that this or that vizier must go, their
method of dispatching him was often bizarre. Murad IV used to
send for the victim, entertain him with a particularly nice feast, and
then hand him a black robe and call in the executioner. A number
of Sultans gave the condemned man an opportunity to save himself
if he could run faster than the executioner from the inner palace to
a certain gate on the Marmara shore. If he won the race (he rarely
did, most viziers being fat and out of training) he was allowed to
keep on going through the gate into exile. Sultan Ahmed I, wish-
ing to dispose of his Grand Vizier, one Nassuf Pasha, sent him two
letters by the hand of the Chief Executioner. The first read, "Fail
not presently upon the receipt hereof, to send me the Seals of my
Empire," the seals being the symbol of his office. Nassuf having
handed over the seals, the Chief Executioner gave him the second
letter which said, "After that thou hast sent me my Seals, send me
thy head by him that shall give thee this note." Michel Baudier,
who reported this story in the West, observes, "This command was
rough and the style of his letter troublesome, yet he must obey.
Nassuf suffered himself to be strangled and the Bostangibassi (Head
Executioner) carried away his head in the view of all his great
family, whereof the least scullions might have broacht him with
their spits. Yet no man moved, seeing the people of the Serrail, and
knowing that it was the Prince's pleasure."

Heads, whether of viziers or of other slaves, were the usual

111

adornment of the Seraglio's second gate, which was called the Gate of the Executioner. Anyone on legitimate business might enter the first gate, but beyond the Gate of the Executioner no one went except by invitation or duress. At this gate, which leads through a wall some twenty feet thick, modern tourists buy their museum tickets and check their umbrellas. There are a few axes on display, but the fountain where the headsman washed up after work is overgrown with weeds, and there is no sign of the "seventy-seven instruments of torture—nails, gimlets, razors, matches for scorching . . . different powders for blinding, clubs for breaking the hands and feet," which a court historian ascribed to Black Ali, Chief Executioner to Murad IV. Of Black Ali's assistants, the record says, "No light shines from their faces, for they are a dark set of people." Foreign ambassadors arriving to present their credentials were customarily kept waiting at this gate for hours and sometimes days in the society of this agreeable crew.

The Chief Executioner, for some obscure reason, was also the Chief Gardener and Chief Helmsman of the Royal Caïque, thus combining in his duties the two most striking characteristics of the Ottoman Turk: extreme ferocity and a touching pleasure in the out-of-doors. The Grand Seraglio was surrounded by gardens— not formal ones like those at Versailles and Schönbrunn, but rambling woods and orchards, like English parks, kept in good order by four thousand gardeners. "Nor indeed doth a Turke at any time shew himself to be so truly pleased, and satisfied in his senses, as he doth . . . in a pleasant garden," reports Ottaviano Bon. "For, he is no sooner come into it but he puts off his uppermost Coat and lays it aside, and upon that his Turbant, then turns up his sleeves and unbuttoneth himself, turning his breast to the wind. . . . Again, sometimes standing upon a high bank to take the fresh air, holding his arms abroad, courting the weather, and sweet air, calling it his soul, his life, and his delight; with whole flowers he stuffes his bosom and decketh his Turbant, shaking his head at their sweet favors; and sometimes singing a song to some pretty flower, by whose name peradventure his mistress is called."

The favorite flower of the Turk was the tulip, once a wild flower of the Asiatic steppes. Holland never heard of tulips until 1562, when a shipment of bulbs arrived from Constantinople; the word "tulip" comes from *tulbend*, meaning "turban," a Turkish nickname for the flower. It was said of Ahmed III, a Sultan of the early eighteenth century, that he valued human life less than a beautiful tulip. He devoted himself to importing new varieties from Europe and the Orient, and, from Venice, glass vases to put them in. At tulip time every spring official business came to a standstill, while Sultan Ahmed put on all-night tulip fêtes in the Seraglio gardens. Guests wore tulip colors, caged birds sang in the tree branches, and here and there among the tulip beds tortoises with candles strapped to their backs provided ambulatory illumination. One night of the fête was reserved for the ladies of the harem, who organized a bazaar at which the Sultan was the only customer. They all looked for candy, hidden Easter-egg style among the flowers, and received prizes handed out by the Chief White Eunuch.

White eunuchs came from among the kidnapped slave children, and, it appears, chose of their own free will to be castrated in order to obtain certain powerful positions in the palace. Eunuchs were believed to be less corruptible than other people (says Ottaviano Bon: "Though not of great courage, yet of the greatest judgment, and fidelity; their minds being set on business, rather than on pleasure") and were thus entrusted with the treasure, the mail, and the secret documents. The governing of the harem was carried on by black eunuchs, most of whom came from the Sudan where they had been captured and castrated as small boys of six or seven. The uglier their faces and persons the more highly they were valued.

A modern view, looking over the roofs of the palace toward the Golden Horn.

Those kidnapped children who showed an aptitude for ferocity were not sent to the Palace School but put into the Janissary Corps. The janissaries were a sort of private army of the Sultan who took the field only when he did and acted as his personal bodyguard. They were first organized in 1330, when the Turks were still living on the plains of Anatolia, and were called *yeni chéri*, meaning "new soldiers." A legend says that a holy man passed his wide sleeve over their heads, blessing them, and for this reason they wore a cap that hung down behind like a sleeve. They were Spartan in their habits, celibate, and forbidden to quarrel with one another. Native Turks and children of former janissaries were not allowed to join the Corps. They were a brave and valuable lot until the great period of Turkish conquests was over and the Sultans became more interested in dallying at home in the Seraglio than in leading troops. Their number swelled from twelve thousand under Suleiman the Magnificent to forty-nine thousand a hundred years later, as more and more captured children entered their ranks and no great wars killed them off. From admirably disciplined assault troops they turned into a rowdy and dangerous mob of hoodlums, always discontented, looting, starting fires, and prone to start revolutions.

Janissaries wore long mustachios but no beards. Their rank was shown by the color of their boots—red, yellow, or black. A high-ranking janissary wore a bird of paradise plume curving down his back as far as his knees. The Corps emblem was a kettle, and the Chief of Janissaries was titled Head Soup-Distributor. Each man wore in his cap a spoon in a brass socket. Every Friday a large delegation of janissaries came to the second court of the Seraglio, just inside the Executioner's Gate, to get their weekly rice allowance, and if they were disgruntled about anything they would turn their kettles upside down and beat on them with their spoons, a warning to those in the inner palace that somebody's head was wanted.

Janissaries were uneducated except in violence and were fanatically conservative. In 1763, when Lord Baltimore passed through Constantinople, he observed that the Corps was still carrying bows and arrows, sabers and lances, having never got used to firearms. Sultan Selim III, in 1807, was dethroned and murdered during a janissary revolt because he had attempted some reforms, among them the introduction of a printing press into Turkey. Turks had been resisting the printing press ever since it had been invented, on the grounds that if the scriptures were printed they wouldn't be scriptures any more.

By 1826, when Mahmud II succeeded in abolishing the Janissaries, there were 135,000 of them. Six Sultans in two and a half centuries had been dethroned or murdered by the Corps that was supposed to guard them. Lady Mary Wortley Montagu, on her visit to Constantinople in 1717, observed that the Grand Seigneur "trembles at a janissary's frown. [The Turks have] none of our harmless calling names! But when a minister here displeases . . . in three hours' time he is dragged even from his master's arms. They cut off his hands, head, and feet, and throw them before the palace gate, with all the respect in the world; while that Sultan (to whome they all profess an unlimited adoration) sits trembling in his apartment, and dare neither defend nor revenge his favourite. This is the blessed condition of the most absolute monarch upon earth, who owns no law but his will." Mahmud II plotted for sixteen years to undermine the power of the janissaries, then provoked them into rebellion and used the regular army to destroy them. Twenty-five thousand janissaries died in three days in Constantinople, and that was the end of the Corps.

It is hardly surprising that the Sultan, the Sublime Turk, at the top of this peculiar political structure, was always eccentric, frequently bloodthirsty, and sometimes totally out of his mind. From his solid-gold cradle on, he was the center of lethal intrigue. While he was heir apparent he was in continual danger of being murdered by his younger brothers, who had everything to gain by his death, since the law of the land, the Law of Fratricide, required that when an heir apparent succeeded to the throne he must destroy all his brothers so that there could be no excuse for civil war. Another curious law, the Law of Succession, was borrowed by medieval Turks from the House of Genghis Khan in the warlike days when a ruler was apt to be killed in battle while still young, leaving only a child heir. This law provided that the inheritance must go first to the eldest member of the royal family and then, on his death, back again to the direct heir. Thus a living brother of the Sultan took precedence over the Sultan's son.

When Mohammed III came to the throne in 1595 he ordered the immediate destruction of his nineteen brothers. As these were all under the age of eleven and had not yet been circumcised, the executioners first circumcised and then strangled them. One child was eating chestnuts when his murderers found him and begged to be allowed to finish, but his request was not granted. It was unlawful to spill royal blood, so the business was done by strangulation, usually by mutes, with a silken bowstring.

Ahmed I, the son of Mohammed III, was the first Sultan to break the Law of Fratricide. He refused to eliminate his brother Mustafa because Mustafa was half-witted, and all half-wits are, according to the Koran, especially beloved of Allah. Instead of killing him, Ahmed had him shut up in a small, two-story building in the inner regions of the harem, which came to be known as the

Cage. When Ahmed died in 1617, Mustafa, under the Law of Succession, inherited the throne. But when it became clear that he was not up to functioning as Sultan, he was put back in the Cage and Ahmed's fourteen-year-old son Osman was enthroned in his place. At once all the civil disorder broke out that the Law of Fratricide had been designed to prevent. The janissaries overturned their kettles, and for six years there was a terrible struggle between factions for Mustafa and factions for Osman. Before order was restored both of them had been murdered.

The next Sultan, Murad IV, who came to the throne at twelve, put things to rights by eliminating four thousand fractious janissaries and closing the coffeehouses, which had become nests of spies and plotters. Prohibition, already a church and state law, he emphasized by pouring boiling lead down the throats of drinkers. He also, for pleasure, used to cut an ass in two with one sword stroke.

This ferocious Sultan was completely under the thumb of his mother, a bloody old lady named Kiusem. Kiusem persuaded Murad not to liquidate his younger brother Ibrahim but to keep him instead in the Cage; so that when Murad died in 1640 Ibrahim succeeded him, and Kiusem continued as Queen Mother and the power behind the throne.

Ibrahim was a homicidal maniac. He had been in the Cage since babyhood and, ever since he had been old enough to realize that he was a younger brother, had lived in daily expectation of the mutes with bowstrings. Therefore, when the viziers came to proclaim him Sultan, the first thing he did was to pile all the furniture in front of the door. Once convinced, however, that he was not to be killed but enthroned, he indulged himself in all of his criminal and crazy whims. He built a kiosk and lined it with sable; he threw gold sequins to the goldfish in the palace lake; he festooned his beard with precious jewels. One day in a fit of pique, he had each of his three hundred concubines put into a sack with a stone at her feet and drowned in the Sea of Marmara. (The story goes that some years later a diver, looking for a submerged wreck, descended into the Marmara and came up almost at once babbling incoherently about hundreds of sacks, held upright by weights at one end, nodding and bowing in the current.) Ibrahim made a bath attendant the General of the Janissaries and an itinerant Arab singer Lord Chamberlain. Even Evliya Effendi, Murad's Boon Companion and a staunch admirer of Sultans, was obliged to write that Ibrahim was "not very intelligent." After eight years of Ibrahim, a janissary revolution overthrew him and put him back in the Cage, where the mutes with bowstrings paid him an overdue visit. One of his sons succeeded to the throne, and the new Queen

Mother very sensibly had the old one strangled and turned over her power to a capable vizier.

In earlier days the royal heirs had gained some knowledge of their empire by fighting at the front or governing distant provinces. But after the middle of the seventeenth century they never left the Cage. One Sultan, who succeeded to the throne after fifty caged years, was unable to speak; another, who had employed his thirty-nine years there in copying and illuminating Korans, begged to be allowed to get on with it. The princes received very little education and what they did receive was apt to come from doctored textbooks. Prince Abdul Aziz, at the beginning of the nineteenth century, studied textbooks in which the Turks had never suffered a military defeat and the French Revolution had never happened. The princes' company was limited to that of eunuchs and women chosen for their barrenness.

Modern Turks, who are extremely proud of their history since 1920, prefer to ignore the seamy history of the Sultans. Because of this, and also because they are relatively new to the idea of tourism and really cannot see why a foreigner would be interested in browsing around any damp old Turkish buildings, the Museum of the Grand Seraglio is not only provocative but provoking. Enough treasure is there—emerald-encrusted coffee cups, plumed fans with diamonds hanging like dew among the plumes, a pure gold throne—to give a hint of the old, vast splendor. There are the Sultans' portraits—grim Sultans, foxy Sultans, obese and mad-eyed Sultans, there are marble balustrades and tattered brocade draperies, and one or two of the fountains that once made the whole palace murmurous with playing water. But the buildings are badly lit, the gardens raggle-taggle, and the few signs and labels maddeningly uninformative. It is as though the old palace still resented intruders and would like to keep them cooling their heels, as visiting ambassadors were kept at the Gate of the Executioner.

In the old days, when the Sultan was ready to grant an audience to a waiting ambassador, a herald cried out cordially, "Let the dogs be fed!" The audience always took place on a day when the Divan (the imperial council) was meeting and the janissaries were to be paid, so that the ambassador, already unstrung by what he had seen in the executioner's quarters, would be overwhelmed by the splendor of the viziers, the bottomlessness of the imperial coffers, and the ferocious appearance of the janissaries. Each vizier arrived at the palace separately, making with his entourage a little parade of his own. The Divan was so numerous that it took from four until ten in the morning to get itself together —all, of course, in a profound hush.

The walls and ceiling of the Hall of the Divan glittered with gold and gems, and the floor was paved with gold, a decorative touch that never failed to stun Western visitors. The Sultan did not appear in this room, but there was (and still is) a latticed bay window high up in its wall which was known as the Eye of the Sultan. "The King's private awful window," it was called. No one in the room below could tell whether His Majesty was there or not.

Sitting on a velvet couch, the ambassador was served pilau, about fifty different and rather monotonous dishes involving mutton or poultry, baklava, and rose-water sherbet, which, if it were summer, was cooled with ice brought by camel caravan from the Asiatic Mount Olympus, two hundred miles to the south. If the Turks wanted to be especially cordial, a brazier filled with burning aloe wood was passed under the ambassador's chin so that he could have the pleasure of saturating his beard with its incense.

Meanwhile, the presents brought by the ambassador from his sovereign were unpacked and paraded around the Court of the Divan for everyone to take stock of. The Venetians always made sure to tuck in, among the glass and cut velvet, some Parmesan cheeses, for cheese was not made in Turkey. Louis XV sent mirrors for the harem. Queen Elizabeth sent Murad III an organ; and to his favorite, Safiyeh, a Venetian woman who had been captured by Turkish pirates, she sent a small picture of herself in a diamond frame, enough cloth of gold for ten dresses, a case of crystal bottles, and some musk. Safiyeh wrote in a thank-you note, "The singular love which we have conceived one toward the other is like to a garden of pleasant birds," and sent Elizabeth some bloomers.

After dining with the viziers, the ambassador and the ranking gentlemen of his party were bundled into robes of silver or gold brocade trimmed with sable, in order to make them presentable enough for the royal eye, and were at last ushered into the audience chamber. This room, called the Throne Room Without (there being a Throne Room Within), stands just inside the Third Gate, or Gate of Happiness. (Gates, since ancient times in the Orient, have been associated with government and the dispensing of justice, which is why the throne room was placed here and why the Ottoman capital city was known as the Sublime Porte, taking this name from that of the main gate of the Seraglio.) The Throne Room Without was even more glittering than the Hall of the Divan, with ropes of pearls dangling from the ceiling and jeweled throne coverings varying in splendor according to the importance of the ambassador being received. An ambassador of Charles II of England, who was probably considered worth a good show, found the Sultan sitting on cloth of gold sewn with diamonds, with his feet, in little white leather shoes soft-soled like a baby's, planted on a green satin rug that was thickly barnacled with gold, pearls, and turquoises. Two pashas led the ambassador forward, pushed his head down until it almost touched the ground, and permitted him to kiss the hem of the Grand Seigneur's brocade sleeve. In response to this His Majesty merely stared at the wall, as he never took any notice of a Christian. If he wished to communicate with him he would do so through a vizier, who would refer to the ambassador's sovereign as "my brother" in order to make clear the Sultan's exalted position among rulers. The audience concluded, the visitors were attended back to their embassy by a great many janissaries and whirling dervishes, all of whom required tips.

The Throne Room Without was as far into the Seraglio as any foreigner or any Turk who did not belong in the palace was supposed to go. Beyond lay the Grand Seigneur's private apartments; the harem; the privy gardens; the quarters of pages and eunuchs; a mosque containing a mantle, a tooth, and some of the beard of the Prophet; and the Sultan's private treasury. All of these regions were so sacrosanct that in 1600 a Venetian who peered at the walls through a spyglass from the other side of the Golden Horn was put to death at once. One of the few outsiders who reached the private apartments and lived to tell about it was an Englishman named Dallam, who was sent by Queen Elizabeth to set up the organ she had given the Sultan. He managed to bribe a eunuch to let him peer through a grille into a courtyard full of harem girls. "At the firste sighte of them I thoughte they had bene young men," he reports, "but when I saw the hare of their heades hange doone on their backes platted together with a tasle of smale pearle . . . and by other plaine tokens I did know them to be women, and verrie prettie ones in deede. Theie wore . . . a little capp . . . faire cheans of pearle . . . and juels in their ears; their coats weare like a souldier's mandilyon, som of red sattan and som of blew . . . britches of . . . fine clothe made of coton woll, as whyte as snow and as fine as lane. . . . Som of them did weare fine cordovan buskins, and some had their leges naked, with a goulde ringe on the smale of her legg. I stood so longe looking upon them that he which had showed me all this kindnes began to be verrie angrie . . . and stamped his fotte to make me give over looking; the which I was verrie lothe to dow, for that sighte did please me wondrous well."

The organ he set up was sixteen feet high and had a clock on top of it with a "holly bushe full of blacke birds and thrushis, which . . . did singe and shake their wynges." When Dallam demonstrated this to the Sultan, His Majesty asked an attendant "yf it would ever doo the lyke againe." The attendant answered that "it would doo the lyke againe at the next houre." "I will see that," said the Grand Seigneur and sat down to wait. As the birds

The imaginary drawing above was made by Anton I. Melling from detailed descriptions of the interior of the harem and its daily activities (from *Voyages Pittoresques*). The other engravings, from William Alexander's *Picturesque Rep-*

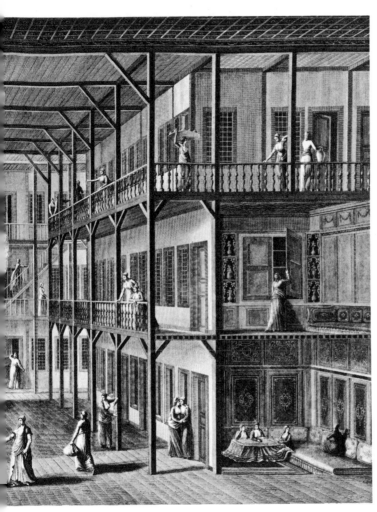

resentations of the Dress and Manner of the Turks,
show Seraglio inhabitants, including women of
the royal harem, the keeper of the bowstring used
for royal executions. and a jannissary, bearing
the gigantic ladle which symbolized his corps.

were adjusted to sing every fourth hour, Dallam, feeling dreadfully ill, had just sixty minutes to make intricate changes in the clock-work. He managed to get the birds in line and caught the next boat back to England.

Clocks were greatly prized in Turkey. They were not allowed to be made there or set up in public places for fear of lessening the importance and authority of the muezzins' five daily calls to prayer. Clockwork toys were coveted even more. Among Mohammed the Conqueror's favorite booty at the taking of Constantinople was a pair of golden lions that roared, and a golden tree, big enough for a man to sit under, full of singing birds. A French merchant in 1685 was able to get a look inside the harem by bribing the Chief Black Eunuch with a mechanical man playing a drum.

The Turks acquired from the Byzantines not only mechanical toys but a good many habits now regarded as typically Turkish: the seclusion of women, the use of eunuchs as palace functionaries, the seclusion and semideification of the Royal Person, strict hier-archy and ceremony at court, and the luxury and fierce intrigue among powerful officials. The early Turkish rulers had been easily accessible to their people; but by the time of Suleiman the Magnifi-cent, in the century after the conquest of Constantinople, the only remnant of the Sultan's ancient accessibility was in his riding out every Friday to the mosque of Aya Sofia (formerly the great church of Saint Sophia). At this time any subject of the realm had the right to present a petition. He did so by writing down his grievance, tying the paper to the end of a long stick, and prostrating himself in the street. When the Sultan rode by on a horse whose mane was tied with diamond tassels, the petitioner, face to the ground, agi-tated the stick in the air and his petition was collected by an attendant.

When the Sultan got back to the palace, dinner would be served. He ate alone and in silence, as nobody was worthy to eat with him. Because of the ban on noise, mutes were his favorite companions. At table he was surrounded with them, and he con-versed with them in sign language, threw them scraps from the table, kicked them, and tossed them gold pieces. He sat at a low revolving table resembling a Lazy Susan and covered with Bulgar-ian leather. According to Ottaviano Bon, who was reporting secondhand but had his information from a Chief White Eunuch, he had a "very rich wrought towel cast before him upon his knees to save his clothes," as he ate with his fingers. "He useth no salt at his Table, neither hath he any Antepaste, but immediately falls aboard the flesh, and having well fed, closeth up his stomach with Bocklava, or some such like thing."

Serving the royal dinner required two hundred waiters. These

arranged themselves in a long line, which extended through courtyards and corridors a hundred yards or so from the kitchen to the
table. The dishes were passed from hand to hand, rapidly and
without the smallest clatter. The royal service was always celadon,
because this porcelain was supposed to have the property of render-
ing poisoned food harmless. Dropping a dish was punishable by
death, not because of the value of the dish but because of the in-
excusable racket, which may explain why the present-day museum
has a vast collection of intact celadon.

After dinner the Grand Seigneur might go for a row in his
seventy-eight-foot caïque. This was propelled at high speed by
twenty-four specially assigned palace pages, who wore loose white
garments and blue caps with red tassels. The Sultan sat in the
stern under a gold-fringed crimson canopy, the only canopy allowed on the Bosporus. An eighteenth-century French ambassador
who tried having one too received word from the Seraglio that
diplomatic relations with France would be null and void until he
got rid of it. Each foreign ambassador was allowed a ten-oar caïque
and might fly his national flag, but he was not allowed to open an
umbrella over his head. He might if he wished, fan himself with a
swan-feather fan.

Six caïques attended the large one bearing the Sultan. In the
second was the Turban Bearer, who held up a turban and inclined
it right and left to save the Sultan the effort of bowing. The oars-
men rowed standing, but the helmsman, who was also the Head
Gardener and Chief Executioner and a very influential pasha, was
allowed to sit in order to handle the rudder. Only he was permitted
to converse with the Sultan as they skimmed along, and while
they spoke, slaves rolled on the bottom of the boat and howled
like dogs so that no one might hear what was being said.

The inner and residential part of the Seraglio was called the
House of Happiness. It is hard to imagine who was happy there—
certainly not the fifteen hundred women of the harem. For most of
them life was like that in a strict boarding school from which there
was never any graduation. Unless they were royal favorites they
slept in dormitories accommodating ten or fifteen pallets on the
floor, under the supervision of an old Moorish woman. Their education was limited to such matters as embroidery and dancing, the
proper manner of bowing before the Sultan, or the playing of the
saz, a long-necked, four-stringed affair that produces a plunking
sound like a banjo. They could read the Koran and could write a
little, although they had nobody to write to, having forever severed
connection with their families. Each woman had one particular
duty in the housekeeping arrangements: the First Mistress of the
Coffee, for instance, took care of handing the Sultan his coffee

when he visited the harem, and wore on her headdress a diamond pin in the shape of a coffeepot. They never went out of the palace except for occasional rides in a closed carriage or caïque. Any men-servants who entered the harem—wood carriers, for example—walked between closed ranks of black eunuchs, and wore long woolen curls hanging down on each side of their faces to act as blinders. A doctor was sometimes allowed in the harem in case of serious illness, but he might examine only his patient's hand and pulse, the rest of her being smothered in quilts. If she was one of the Sultan's concubines, a silken veil covered her hand.

Many of these women lived and died without so much as a smile from His Majesty; others were smiled at, and for this reason pro-moted to the rank of *gözde,* meaning "in the eye" (of the Sultan) but never got any further than that; others were invited to the royal couch one or more times, which made them *ikbal,* or royal favorites, and entitled them to an increase in jewels and silk dresses and a private bedroom; and at the top of the ladder were the *kadin,* the first four concubines who produced children. The Sultan by tradi-tion did not marry, but a *kadin* had the rank of wife except that no dower was settled on her, as is required in the Moslem marriage contract. The chief reason for this arrangement was to save money for the state, since a suitable dower for a Sultan's wife would have seriously embarrassed the treasury. Suleiman the Magnificent defied tradition and married his favorite, Roxelana; and it was she who moved the women's quarters, formerly in another part of the city, into the Seraglio. When Suleiman died, Roxelana became the power behind the throne of her son Selim the Sot, and for a hundred and fifty years thereafter a succession of ruthless, conniving queen mothers were the real rulers of Turkey. They were abetted by a verse in the Koran which reads, "Paradise is under the feet of thy Mother." Ottoman "momism" was particularly unattractive be-cause these old ladies were not only dominating but as evil as could be. They had to be evil or they would have been trampled in the general rush of some fifteen hundred women for the most powerful position in the world.

In selecting a concubine, a Sultan held a regular weekly levee at which the virgins of the harem were brought in for his inspec-tion; he dropped a handkerchief at the feet of the one who pleased him most, indicating that she was *gözde* and might hope for a summons to the royal bedchamber. When and if this came, she was dressed in silk and jewels and perfumed with ambergris, with kohl on her eyes and henna on her fingernails, and conducted to the Sultan by the Chief Black Eunuch all in strict secrecy so that the other women would not be waiting to scratch her eyes out the moment she got back. The Sultan's bed had wrought-silver bedposts topped with crystal lions holding in their teeth a gold cloth canopy. He liked the idea of owning a bed, like European rulers, but he slept, as his ancestors did in their tents, on a mattress spread on the floor. Two old Moorish women stood at his head with burning torches so that he might have light to say his beads at the last and the first hours of prayer, as the Koran frowns on praying in the dark. "Thus he rests," soliloquized Baudier, "which troubles all Europe, disquiets Asia and afflicts Africa."

A concubine arriving to spend the night was required to enter the bed from the foot, inching her way up under the covers until she lay level with the Sultan. This performance was also expected of husbands of the Sultan's daughters. These princesses, who wore a silver dagger at their belts to remind their consorts of who outranked whom, were in no demand at all as brides, for their husbands had to take orders from them, and gained no special familiarity with their father-in-law. Children of such unions were not allowed at court at all, and the princesses' dowries could not be inherited by husband or children but reverted to the sultanate, as, indeed, did all the wealth of even the greatest pashas in this slave state.

The strange life of the Grand Seraglio began to languish after the destruction of the janissaries and the partial Europeanization of the Sultans. A new, elaborate palace was built on the Bosporus, and after 1851 the old Seraglio was used only to house the harems of Sultans who had died. One of the last official events there took place in 1909, after Abdul Hamid II had been deposed and forcibly retired to Adrianople together with fifteen concubines, a guard of eunuchs, and his favorite cat. A public notice appeared in the newspapers, stating that anyone having a relative who was a member of the Imperial Harem might, by calling at the Seraglio, reclaim her. Telegrams bearing this news were sent to the headmen of villages in the Caucasus, since many of the women had come from there.

On an appointed day the entire harem, numbering nearly twelve hundred, was assembled without veils in a large hall, while hundreds of Caucasian mountaineers and other Christian people from outposts of the Turkish Empire filed through, seeking to recognize in these elegant ladies their daughters and sisters. Not all of the women were claimed or wanted to be. Some had been spoken for by rich pashas who were anxious for beautiful and delicately bred wives; some nobody came for; some quailed at the prospect of a peasant's life and chose to spend the rest of their days in reduced but genteel circumstances there in the old Seraglio, which thus ended as an old ladies' home.

Bibliography

Besides guidebooks, contemporary newspapers, and magazines, the following sources have proved useful:

LUDWIG'S DREAM CASTLES

Alexander, Leo. "The Commitment and Suicide of King Ludwig II of Bavaria." *The American Journal of Psychiatry*, Vol. III, No. 2, August, 1954

Chapman-Huston, Desmond. *Bavarian Fantasy, The Story of Ludwig II*. London, 1954

Hiermeis, Theodor. *Der König Speist*. Munich, 1953

Kreisel, Heinrich. *The Castles of Ludwig II of Bavaria*. Munich

Richter, Werner. *Ludwig, König vön Bayern*. Munich, 1939

A HABITABLE MONUMENT

Blenheim Palace, by David Green (London, 1958), is the definitive work on the history of Blenheim Palace. Other useful sources are:

Churchill, Winston. *Marlborough, His Life and Times*. London, 1933-38

Colville, Mrs. Arthur. *Duchess Sarah; being the Social History of the Times of Sarah, Duchess of Marlborough*. London, 1904

Kronenberger, Louis. *Marlborough's Duchess*. New York, 1958

Summerson, John. *Architecture in Britain, 1530-1830*. London, 1958

Whistler, Laurence. *The Imagination of Vanbrugh and his Fellow Artists*. London, 1954

"A CLUSTER OF SOAP BUBBLES"

Calvert, Albert F. *The Alhambra*. London, 1906

Gautier, Theophile. *Travels in Spain. (Complete Works, Vol. III).* Translated by F. C. de Sumichrast. London, 1909

Hitti, Philip K. *History of the Arabs*. 7th ed. New York, 1960

Hole, Edwyn. *Andalus: Spain Under the Muslims*. London, 1959

Irving, Washington. *Tales of the Alhambra*. 1832

Prieto-Moreno, F. *Los Jardines de Granada*. Madrid, 1952

Sordo, Enrique. *Moorish Spain*. Translated by Ian Michael. London, 1963

THE EMPEROR'S FOLLY

Aurigemma, Salvatore. "Lavori nel Canopo di Villa Adriana." In several issues of *Bolletino d'Arte*. Rome 1954-56

Carcopino, J. *Daily Life in Ancient Rome*. London, 1956

Clark, Eleanor. *Rome and a Villa*. New York, 1952

Grant, Michael. *The World of Rome*. London, 1960

Hansen, Erik. *La "Piazza d'Oro" e la sua Cupola*. Denmark, 1960

Kähler, Heinz. *Hadrian und Seine Villa bei Tivoli*. Berlin, 1950

MacKendrick, Paul. *The Mute Stones Speak*. New York, 1960

Winnefeld, Hermann. *Die Villa des Hadrian bei Tivoli*. Berlin, 1950

PALACE IN THE SUN

Bowring, Sir John. *The Kingdom and People of Siam*. London, 1857

Child, Jacob T. *The Pearl of Asia*. London, 1892

Finlayson, George. *The Mission to Siam and Hue, the Capital of Cochin China in the Years 1821-22*. London, 1826

Graham, Walter Armstrong. *Siam*. 1912

Hutchinson, E. W. *Adventures in Siam in the Seventeenth Century*. 1940

Moffat, Abbot Low. *Mongkut, the King of Siam*. Ithaca, N.Y., 1961

Norman, Sir Henry. *The Peoples and Politics of the Far East*. London, 1895

Smith, Malcolm. *A Physician at the Court of Siam*. London, 1947

Wales, H. G. Q. *Siamese State Ceremonies*. London, 1931

William, Prince of Sweden. *In the Lands of the Sun*. 1915

Wood, W. A. R. *Land of Smiles*. Bangkok, 1935

"THE VERY PEARL OF THE REALM"

Special acknowledgment is due to John Dent, whose *The Quest for Nonsuch*, London, 1962, covers the subject comprehensively. Other useful sources are:

Aikin, Lucy. *Memoirs of the Court of Queen Elizabeth*. London, 1818

Biddle, Martin. "The Palace Which Henry VIII Built and Charles II's Mistress Demolished," *Illustrated London News*, May 28, 1960

Buxton, John. *Elizabethan Taste*. London, 1963

Evelyn, John. *Diary*.

Fastnedge, Ralph. *English Furniture Styles from 1500 to 1830*. London, 1962

Pepys, Samuel. *Diary*.

Pevsner, Nikolaus. *An Outline of European Architecture*. Harmondsworth, England, 1942

Platter, Thomas. *Travels in England*. Translated by Clare Williams. London, 1937

Willis, Cloudesley. *A Short History of Ewell and Nonsuch*. Epsom, England, 1932

THE MARBLE COTTAGES

Andrews, Wayne. *The Vanderbilt Legend*. New York, 1941

———. *Architecture, Ambition, and Americans*. New York, 1955

Bourget, Paul. *Outremer: Impressions of America*. New York, 1895

Downing, Antoinette F., and Scully, Vincent J., Jr. *The Architectural Heritage of Newport*. New York, 1952

James, Henry. *The American Scene*. New York, 1907

Nichols, C. W. *The Ultra-Fashionable Peerage*. New York, 1904

Van Rensselaer, Mrs. May King. *Newport, The Social Capital*. New York, 1905

Wecter, Dixon. *Saga of American Society*. New York, 1937

THE GRAND SERAGLIO

Baltimore, Lord Frederick Calvert. *Tour to the East in the Years 1763 and 1764.* London, 1767

Baudier, Michel. *The History of the Imperial Estate of the Grand Seigneurs.* English translation. London, 1635

Bon, Ottaviano. *The Grand Seraglio.* Translated by Robert Withers. London, 1650

Busbecq, Ogier de. *The Turkish Letters of Ogier de Busbecq, 1554-62.* Translated by Edward Seymour Foster. Oxford, 1927

Creasy, Sir Edward. *Turkey.* Rev. and ed. by A. C. Coolidge and W. Harold Claflin. Philadelphia, 1906

Evliya, Effendi. *Travels.* Translated by J. von Hammer. London, 1834-46

McCullagh, Francis. *The Fall of Abdul Hamid.* London, 1910

Menavino, Giovanni Antonio. *Trattato de Costumi et Vita de Turchi.* Florence, 1548

Miller, Barnette. *Beyond the Sublime Porte.* New Haven, Conn., 1936

Montagu, Lady Mary Wortley. *Letters from the Levant.* London, 1717

Penzer, Norman Mosley. *The Harem.* London, 1936

Piazzi, Adriana (Leila Hanoum). *Le Harem Impérial.* Paris, 1878

Rosedale, H. G. *Queen Elizabeth and the Levant Company.* London, 1904

Tavernier, Jean Baptiste. *A New Relation of an Inner View of the Grand Seigneur's Seraglio.* London, 1677

White, Charles. *Three Years in Constantinople; or Domestic Manners of the Turks in 1844.* London, 1846